Pippa Kendrick

free-from food for family & friends

Over a hundred delicious recipes,
all gluten free, dairy free & egg free

HarperCollins*Publishers*

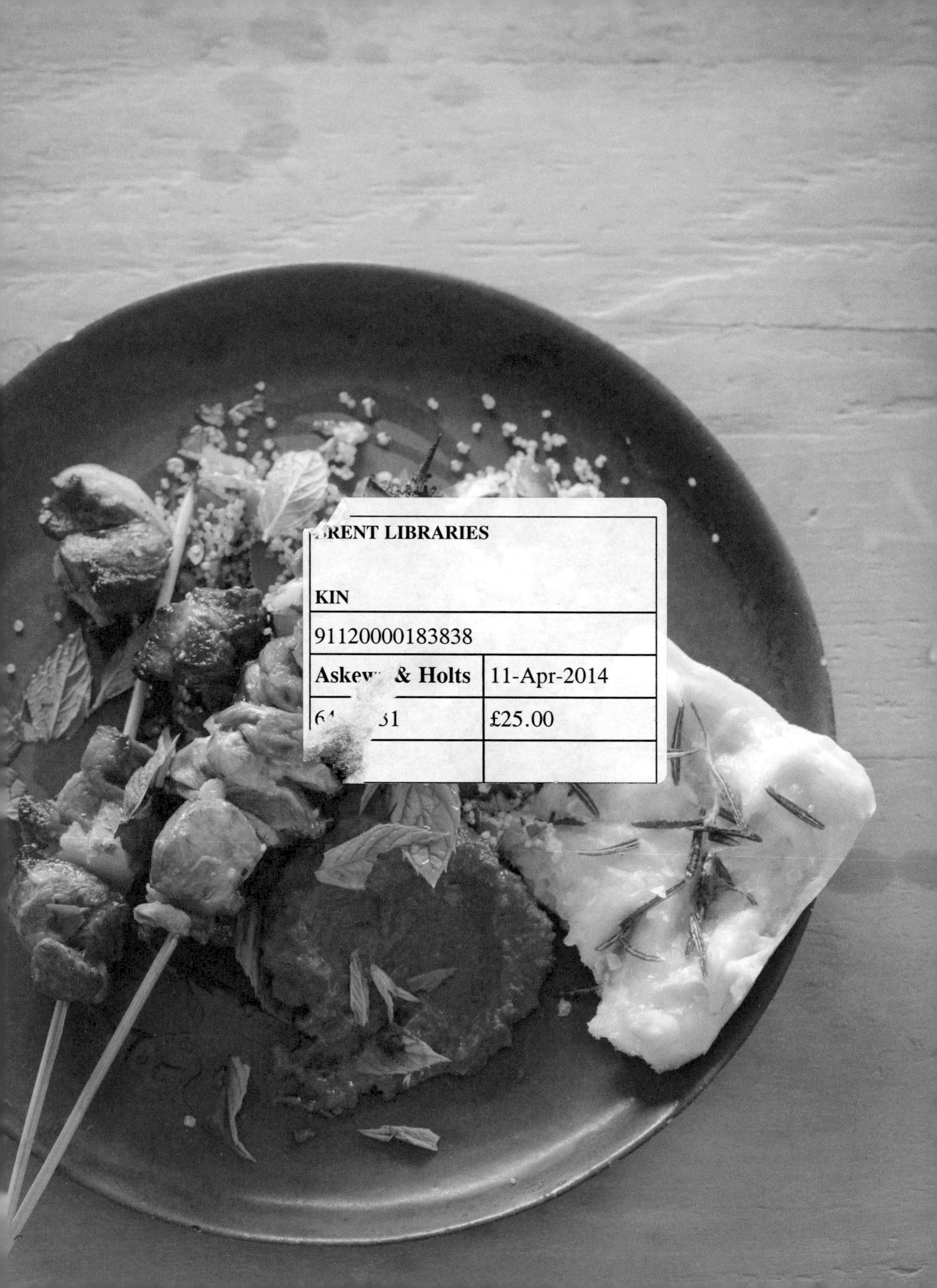

foreword
6

introduction
10

cooking notes
13

breakfasts
16

elevenses
30

al fresco
50

light lunches
72

lazy Afternoons
92

Family favourites
114

WEEKNIGHT food
132

Fireside suppers
152

WeekeNd feasts
174

ProPer Puddings
200

glossary
224

contents by course
235

index
236

thanks
240

foreword

Having grown up in the countryside on a little winding lane with an apple farm next door, I have always loved everything food-related. We were treated to freshly pressed juice every day from the farm; we had eggs from our free-range chickens and vegetables from my mum's abundant vegetable garden. She was passionate about vegetarian and wholefood cooking and my dad was a firm believer in locally sourced and reared meats, so I was raised on a wide variety of different foods. Having travelled extensively, my parents embraced unusual flavours and exotic spices; you were just as likely to find fragrant curries or Greek mezze on our kitchen table as you were apple crumble or chicken and mushroom pie. Having spent many years living in Hong Kong, my grandparents also made sure that Chinese food was our 'Sunday' staple when we visited them for lunch. We ate a pretty unusual range of foods for the early 1980s, all of it made from scratch and all of it delicious, whatever its provenance. So I was lucky to be surrounded by wonderful and exciting food throughout my childhood. But I also had a severe intolerance to dairy produce – one that was never diagnosed at the time. From around the age of five, I suffered from a painfully swollen face and limbs, aching legs, itchy skin, constant tummy aches, chronic insomnia, exhaustion and a general feeling of being uncomfortable in my own body. I did not look and feel as healthy as a child of my age and lifestyle should. But, as was the way of things in those days, nothing was really made of it. My symptoms and illnesses were never considered together as a whole and, being a child, I didn't know any different. By the time I was a teenager, the symptoms had become out of control: I suffered terrible abdominal pains and visited the doctor repeatedly, only to be loosely diagnosed with indigestion, regardless of the symptoms. I was almost continuously uncomfortable and, looking back, I wonder why I didn't insist that more was done. I can only suppose that I was so used to feeling 'sick and tired' that it had become the norm for me; I certainly never put it down to the food I was eating. We were an epicurean household – no processed food for us – and there seemed little chance that the two things were related.

Stop forward another few years and at university, aged 20, I still suffered from ill health. It was a chance examination by a private doctor (I had to pass a medical exam in order to apply for a visa to study abroad) that would have long-lasting consequences. After looking at my notes, the doctor questioned me about my long history of stomach problems. He booked me in for an ultrasound later that day and within minutes of the scan told me I would need urgent abdominal surgery. Unbeknown

to me, years of eating foods I was intolerant to had taken their toll on my digestive system. Pigment stones, sometimes known as calcium stones, had formed and clogged up both my gall bladder and bile duct, and they would have to be removed immediately.

A few days later, I went into hospital for what I thought would be a routine operation. I would not be discharged for months. Due to a hefty dose of bad luck and mismanagement, what should have been straightforward became near fatal. Symptoms were misdiagnosed and I was subjected to multiple operations that themselves went wrong, leaving me bed-bound and with a badly damaged digestive system that would never be the same again.

It was, as you can imagine, a shattering experience and something that even now I try not to dwell upon. But it was what came next that had the greatest impact on my life subsequently. After almost a year of convalescing, I was mobile once again and could sleep comfortably and eat proper food, the only difference being that I now had to avoid not just dairy produce, but anything with wheat, eggs, soya or yeast in it. My body simply could not digest anything containing these foods. If I did eat something I had become intolerant to, my reactions were so severe that on a number of occasions I ended up back in hospital – which I was rather keen to avoid!

So at just 22 years old, I needed to adopt an entirely new way of life. Everything had to change, from what I ate to how I cooked it. I chose not to be defeated by the restrictions imposed upon me, but to embrace them. I've always loved food and I wanted to continue to enjoy it without feeling constrained. But ten years ago few recipe books were available for people with food intolerances. I was determined to find food that could feed me, fuel me and help to heal me, yet still taste good. Surely there was a way of creating delicious, intolerance-friendly dishes?

This is where it all started. I called upon my experience of eating vibrant, natural wholefoods since childhood and took inspiration from various cooking methods – using different techniques and experimenting with a whole range of ingredients. In my attempts to recreate the taste and texture of 'intolerant' foodstuffs, I focused on seasonal produce and explored different flavours until I felt I had achieved lovely 'free-from' dishes that anyone, food intolerant or not, would find delicious.

It's been an interesting journey since those first few tentative months, and in that time I've been fortunate enough to create my blog, The Intolerant Gourmet, and publish my first book, with the same title. In one sense, I'm incredibly grateful for what I have been through, as I wouldn't be doing what I love if it wasn't for that. I have also come to realise that the food intolerances I have, and the way that they came about, are perhaps a little extreme in comparison to other people's. But I firmly believe that however severe your food sensitivities are, they needn't restrict you. Eating good food should be a pleasure, one to be shared with the people you love and, most importantly, something to be celebrated. I hope that this book can be a part of that celebration, and provide an abundance of delicious 'free-from' food for everyone to enjoy.

introduction

The process of discovering, adjusting to – often recovering from – and then learning to live with food intolerances and allergies can feel like a gruelling ordeal. It's an experience that changes the way you live, how you feel physically and certainly the way in which you eat. In my first book, *The Intolerant Gourmet*, I endeavoured to show you how easy it can be to cook for people suffering from food intolerances. I gave you a seasonally led collection of my favourite allergen-free recipes and opened up my own pantry to prove that it takes only a handful of natural ingredients to adapt and recreate your favourite meals.

In this, my second book, *Free-From Food for Family & Friends*, I follow the same philosophy, with over a hundred delicious new intolerance-friendly recipes, all 100 per cent free from gluten, dairy produce, eggs, soya or yeast. I still believe in cooking by the seasons and cannot encourage you enough to look in your local markets and greengrocers to see what's fresh and plentiful, but I also understand that day-to-day life is not always so straight-forward. Even without factoring in food intolerances, family, work and the increasingly fast pace of life can leave you with less and less time to focus on cooking. But I believe cooking and eating should be a bonding experience – a time for family and friends to come together, an experience to share and indulge in. Whether it's a quick breakfast, a picnic in the sunshine, a cosy supper on a rainy night or a celebratory meal, sitting down to eat should always be a pleasure. Food sensitivities or time constraints need not get in the way, which is why *Free-From Food for Family & Friends* is about food for all the family, to enjoy at any time of day, any day of the week and every day of the year.

The good thing about cooking from scratch is that fresh, 'real' ingredients are infinitely better for you: physically, emotionally and medically. Creating meals for family and friends is also one of life's simple pleasures and needn't be difficult. Even if you only make a batch of lemon shortbread instead of buying a packet of biscuits, you'll see the benefits at once: from the therapeutic mixing of the ingredients, the sweet aroma of the biscuits as they bake wafting through your home and then that wonderful first bite, seeing the pleasure on other people's faces as you offer them a treat, and the security of knowing that you can name every single ingredient that went into that shortbread. Those reasons and more go a little way to explaining why cooking for your family and friends is so important.

Important, and pleasurable; and I promise you that every recipe in this book is about pleasure ... It might be that chocolate tart you've been craving for months, or possibly

years, but have been forced to shun, or the chicken nuggets you know your children would also love. Or maybe it's the granola and yoghurt you've missed being able to eat for breakfast, or the fluffy pancakes for a weekend indulgence. Perhaps it's brownies you've been longing to treat yourself to. Maybe it's just the simple, quick and tasty pasta suppers you miss, or the cups of tea and freshly baked cakes you would like to serve friends. How about soothing ice cream on a hot summer's day, freshly baked savoury muffins for a packed lunch or a huge feast of breads, meats and treats at a family get-together? Whether you're looking for a lazy weekend breakfast with a loved one, a little bit of weekend baking with the children or a platter of delights to share with friends, *Free-From Food for Family & Friends* has something to offer, whether you suffer from a food intolerance or not. What's important is that it's all good food, packed full of flavour, easy to cook and, most of all, something that everyone will enjoy.

Embracing your food intolerances is the best thing you can do for both your mind and body. Once you have moved past the struggle of feeling unwell and adjusting your diet, you will begin to feel healthier and happier. You will also discover the abundance of foods you can eat, from naturally gluten-free grains to dairy-free milks and a whole array of meats, fruits and vegetables. I promise you that there is not one recipe, dish or meal that cannot be adapted, created or bettered by making it intolerance friendly. There are multiple ways to cook the foods you love without feeling that you're missing out, and this book aims to show you just how easy that can be.

I have developed recipes using traditional and modern techniques, classic pairings and fresh flavours, to show you how delicious and simple intolerance-friendly cooking can be for you and your family. So dive in and start

creating delectable 'free-from' dishes today. You can browse and cook by chapter – each one devoted to a method and mealtime that suits you. Quick breakfasts, simple week-night suppers and something suitable for the children's tea are all here, along with al fresco meals, cosy winter suppers and dishes fit for a feast.

The chapters are just a rough guide, of course – you can make the dishes for other meals and at different times of the year – so if you prefer to browse for recipes by type, simply turn to Contents by Course (see page 235). You'll also find a comprehensive Glossary of all the intolerance-friendly foods and products used, in addition to a few recipes for basic items (such as stock or apple purée) that you might prefer to make yourself (see pages 224–33). The aim is to offer you as simple a layout as possible, so that you can find what you want, when you want it, leaving you free for the more important things in life – such as relaxing with friends and family over the delicious meals you've created.

Pippa x

It is difficult to source recipes that are suitable for people suffering from multiple food intolerances, and finding dishes that you can actually eat, let alone enjoy, may start to feel like a challenge. I've created this book for just that reason; I pride my recipes on catering for a range of food intolerances: each dish is completely free from gluten, dairy produce, eggs, soya and yeast. By offering you over a hundred tasty dishes, my aim is to take the struggle and confusion out of selecting the right ingredients so you can focus on preparing and eating delicious food.

Of course, some of you may need to eliminate only one or two foods from your diet. In such cases, it is possible to adapt my recipes to your needs. You could replace the dairy-free margarine in a recipe for butter, for instance, or egg replacer with real eggs in a like-for-like manner; so if the recipe called for 150ml of rice milk, you could use 150ml of cow's milk instead, and if you prefer to use real eggs, then you just need to bear in mind that the ratio is 1 teaspoon of egg replacer plus 2 tablespoons of water for every real egg. That being said, all of my recipes are developed and tested for multiple food intolerances and work perfectly without standard ingredients. You'll find that my fluffy Apple Pancakes with Cinnamon-Roasted Fruit (see page 24) don't need any eggs to

bind them, and my Apple and Blackberry Pie and vanilla custard (see pages 206 and 213) lack nothing in flavour or texture, despite not containing gluten or dairy produce.

The ingredients specified in each recipe have been carefully selected with the whole dish in mind, hence the best results come when you follow the instructions exactly. Therefore if I specify ground flaxseed or apple purée in my baking instead of eggs, it is because they not only help bind the mixture, but also add a texture and flavour that is integral to the dish. I hope you'll find that my recipes as they stand are delectable enough without any revision, though experimentation for pleasure should always be encouraged!

Each recipe in this book is clearly marked as gluten, dairy, egg, soya and yeast free. If a recipe is dairy, egg and meat free, it is labelled as vegan, too. Over 95 per cent of the recipes here are either totally nut free or can be made without nuts, but please note that I do use nuts in a small number of my recipes. Sometimes the key to cooking without dairy produce and eggs is recreating familiar textures. Nuts, especially cashew nuts, can be integral to this: they are indispensable in making my Garlic and Herb Cashew Cream Cheese (see page 56), for example. That said, I have offered a nut-free alternative to the majority of those recipes that include nuts, and each recipe is clearly labelled in any case so that you don't have to worry. While I appreciate that neither sesame seeds nor pine nuts are technically a type of nut, a large number of people allergic to nuts are also allergic to these, according to Allergy UK. For that reason, I have also provided nut-free options for recipes that contain either sesame seeds or pine nuts. Some may query my use of coconut, but coconuts – despite their name – are actually entirely nut free and hence perfect in allergen-free baking and for creating creamy-textured dishes.

a few cooking tips I've learned along the way

Toasting nuts and seeds
Where possible, I like to toast these in the oven rather than on the hob, as toasting in the oven gives an even colour and a much richer, nuttier flavour. I do concede that in those recipes where the oven is not otherwise used, it may seem preferable to toast nuts and seeds in a heavy-based pan on the hob. I leave it to you to choose your favourite way.

Using natural oils rather than margarine
In this book, I have chosen to focus more on using natural oils in baking than dairy-free margarine. That is not to say that I don't still use or favour dairy-free margarine (indeed, it's included in a number of recipes here), though I always ensure it is non-hydrogenated and trans-fat free. It's more that I increasingly use natural oils – sunflower, coconut, rapeseed, to name but a few – as I find that they give a wonderful quality of crumb, taste and texture to my baking. If you'd like to experiment with using oils instead of margarine in your cooking, then a good

rule of thumb is to reduce the quantity of margarine used in the recipe by a third. That will be the amount of oil you then need.

Grating vegetables for use in baking
Although using a food processor to grate vegetables may be easier, I strongly recommend that you do it by hand instead. Vegetables tend to become much damper when grated in a food processor, and this increased water content will affect the rise and crumb of whatever it is that you are baking.

Making allergen-free shortcrust pastry
Making this sort of pastry is actually very easy, but there are a few key tips that can really help you along the way.

Always roll out the pastry between two sheets of cling film or greaseproof paper, as this will stop the pastry from sticking. Gluten-free pastry can be notoriously difficult to handle and rolling it out in this way makes it much more manoeuvrable.

There is no need to chill this pastry – you can make it, roll it out and bake it in one go – and there is no need to bake it blind either, though you can place it on a preheated baking sheet in the oven, if you are nervous about the base of your pastry getting soggy.

If you do want to make the pastry in advance, it will keep for up to five days if stored in the fridge and wrapped in cling film. The only caveat is that you should take it out and bring it up to room temperature before attempting to roll it out, as it will crumble if it's too cold.

Baking biscuits and cookies
In the recipes for biscuits and cookies, you'll see that two baking sheets are specified for cooking 12 or more items, with the instruction that the sheets are swapped around roughly

halfway through cooking to ensure the whole batch bakes evenly. Don't worry if you have only one baking sheet, however; just cook the biscuits in two batches.

Cooking in the oven

The simple truth is that the builders of today's ovens don't seem to worry too much about producing machines with a standard temperature range, hence one oven's 180°C could be another's 170°C. Because of this, as well as the cooking time I always give an indication of how the finished dish should look, feel or smell, using phrases like 'until golden and fragrant' or 'until lightly risen and pulling away from the sides'. While investing in an oven thermometer will certainly help, your eyes and other senses are always the best judge when baking. That said, if you are using a fan oven, please reduce the temperature given in the recipe by 20°C (70°F).

a few notes on ingredients

Meat and fish

I am a firm believer in using the best-quality ingredients that you can buy, just as I am very much on the side of eating seasonally. Yet it can be hard, in the flurry of our everyday lives, to stay rigorously true to this and I, for one, do not always buy produce that's in season or organically produced. The exception to this is meat and fish; I highly recommend that you buy free-range or organic meat or sustainable fish wherever possible. Not only is the provenance much more trustworthy, but the meat tastes far better, too.

Fresh herbs

A 'small bunch' means around 7g in weight or half your average 'packet' from the supermarket; a 'large bunch' implies around 15g or one 'packet'.

Stocks

Please refer to the Glossary (see page 232) for a recipe for chicken and vegetable stock and for good-quality gluten- and yeast-free stock powders.

Teaspoon/tablespoon measures

1 teaspoon = 5ml; 1 tablespoon = 15ml

breakfasts

banana,
maple & oat smoothie
coconut &
mango smoothie
granola with
banana 'yoghurt'
peanut butter
& banana muffins
apple pancakes with
cinnamon-roasted fruit
potato farls
maple syrup scones
chickpea bread
for toast & jam
hot-smoked salmon kedgeree
with cashew sauce

banana,
maple & oat smoothie

nut-free
option

This is an incredibly simple and quick breakfast drink, but ambrosial all the same. I can think of nothing nicer than having this for breakfast each morning, especially in the warmer months. The combination of the oats and bananas provides a sustaining boost, while the maple syrup, almond milk and cinnamon add a sweet and creamy note. It is, essentially, a healthy milkshake to begin the day – and what could be better, or easier?

contains nuts   nut-free option   gluten free   vegan   soya free   yeast free

Serves 1

1 frozen banana
250ml almond milk (or other
    dairy-free milk for
    a nut-free option)
30g gluten-free
    porridge oats
1 tsp maple syrup
A pinch of ground cinnamon

Place all of the ingredients except the cinnamon in a blender and blitz until completely smooth. Sprinkle with the cinnamon and serve.

*To boost both flavour and nutrient content
you could try adding 1 teaspoon of Maca
or Lucuma powder to your smoothie...*

coconut &
mango smoothie

This is another super-quick breakfast option, totally suited to the warmer months of the year when you want to wake yourself up with something fruity and refreshing. The coconut milk (the carton variety rather than the tinned, the former being thinner and more milk–like, the latter creamier and better suited for cooking) provides a rich base, the frozen banana thickens the mixture and the fresh mango and strawberries add just the right amount of sweetness. I highly recommend it for a bright and boosting beginning to the day. If you want to make this for more than one person, simply multiply the quantities specified in the recipe.

---

nut free   *gluten free*   *vegan*   *soya free*   *yeast free*

Serves 1

6 fresh strawberries
½ fresh or frozen mango
½ frozen banana
250ml coconut milk

Hull the strawberries and slice and skin the mango (if using the fresh variety). Place all of the ingredients in a blender and blitz until smooth. Serve immediately.

nut-free
option

granola with
banana 'yoghurt'

Granola, to my mind, is the bedrock of a good breakfast, served with either cold rice milk, hot almond milk, a dollop of fruit compote or some sweet stewed apples. Offer it to me in the depths of winter or the bright buzzy mornings of summer and I am a happy girl. This particular recipe is a blend of my favourite ingredients. Well balanced – nutty, not too sweet but with a hint of cinnamon – it's a firm favourite in my house and will keep for weeks in an airtight jar or container, if you can ration it for that long! The banana 'yoghurt' is so simple, you may question its presence here, but it's such a great way of creating a creamy-tasting yet dairy-free topping for your cereal that I just had to include it! I recommend using one ripe banana per person and serving it immediately, as the mixture can discolour if left too long. A bowl of granola with a little chopped apple or plum on top or a scattering of blueberries and a generous pouring of banana yoghurt is a delicious way to start the day. If you want to make the granola nut free, simply swap the 100g of pecans for the same quantity of pumpkin seeds or a mixture of pumpkin seeds and coconut flakes – they will add the same nutty bite.

contains nuts   nut-free option   gluten free   vegan   soya free   yeast free

Makes about 1kg

100ml maple syrup
4 tbsp coconut oil
100g shelled pecans (or
    pumpkin seeds and/or
    coconut flakes for
    a nut-free option)
250g gluten-free
    porridge oats
A pinch of sea salt flakes
150g sunflower seeds
1 heaped tsp ground
    cinnamon
150g pitted dates (Medjool
    are my favourite – by far
    the juiciest and sweetest)
150g mixed sultanas
    or raisins
100g ground flaxseed

For the banana 'yoghurt'
(serves 1)
1 ripe banana
Juice of ½ orange or 2 tbsp
    of fruit juice

Preheat the oven to 180°C (350°F), gas mark 4, and line a large baking sheet with baking parchment.

Pour the maple syrup and coconut oil into a small saucepan and heat-v gently over a low heat until melted and combined. Meanwhile, chop the pecans (if using) into small pieces, scatter on a baking tray and roast in the oven, turning occasionally to make sure they don't burn, for 6–8 minutes or until lightly toasted and fragrant. Remove from the oven and set aside to cool down.

Next, mix the oats, salt and sunflower seeds (adding the pumpkin seeds and/or coconut flakes, if using) in a large bowl. Pour over the melted oil and syrup and stir in until the oats are well coated in the mixture. Spread the mixture over the lined baking sheet, sprinkle with the cinnamon and bake in the oven for 25 minutes or until lightly golden, mixing the oats up and then levelling them out on the baking sheet every 5 minutes or so to ensure they cook evenly. Once toasted, remove from the oven and set aside to cool down.

While the granola is cooling, roughly chop the dates and mix them with the sultanas, flaxseed and toasted pecans. Add to the granola and stir together until evenly mixed, then transfer to an airtight jar or container.

To make the 'yoghurt', place the banana and fruit juice in a blender or food processor and blitz until completely smooth. Pour over the granola and serve at once.

peanut butter
& banana muffins

nut-free option

Muffins, in the American sense of the word, can be an incredibly sweet affair, sitting somewhere between cake and bread. This delicious version balances happily between sweet and savoury: the intense flavour of ripe bananas is complemented by the crunch of the peanuts, while the flaxseed adds a wholesome, malty touch, making the muffins perfect for serving at breakfast with a cup of tea and perhaps some fruit compote on the side. They're also rather lovely served in the afternoon and are ideal for picnics or trips away. Most muffins are at their best served warm from the oven, but these, thanks in part to the bananas, retain their moistness and so can last for up to three days if stored in an airtight container.

contains nuts   nut-free option   gluten free   vegan   soya free   yeast free

Makes 8 large muffins

4 tbsp ground flaxseed
¼ tsp gluten-free baking powder
3 large ripe bananas
125ml sunflower or rapeseed oil
100g soft light brown sugar
3 tbsp crunchy peanut butter (or sunflower seed butter for a nut-free option – see the Glossary, pages 232–3)
225g gluten-free plain flour (ideally Doves Farm)
1 tsp bicarbonate of soda

Equipment
You will need a 12-hole muffin tin for this recipe

Preheat the oven to 200°C (400°F), gas mark 6, and line the muffin tin with muffin cases or papers.

Mix the ground flaxseed and baking powder with 6 tablespoons of water and leave this to stand while you prepare the other ingredients – the flax mixture will absorb the water and swell up to form a paste.

Place the bananas in a large bowl and, using a fork, mash until smooth. Pour in the sunflower or rapeseed oil, then add the sugar, peanut butter (or sunflower seed butter) and flax mixture and beat together until well combined. Sift in the flour and bicarbonate of soda and stir together until blended.

Spoon the muffin mixture into the cases or papers, filling these two-thirds full, and bake in the oven for 20–25 minutes or until slightly risen, golden and fragrant. Remove from the oven and leave to stand in the tin for a few minutes, then either serve warm or transfer to a wire rack to cool down completely.

apple pancakes with cinnamon-roasted fruit

These thick and fluffy pancakes bear more than a passing resemblance to the American versions you see piled high with maple syrup and crispy bacon on top, and they do indeed work beautifully when served like that. Here, I've paired them with some roasted, cinnamon-spiced fruit. Wrapping the fruit in baking parchment helps to keep it moist, while tying the parcels with string both looks pretty and keeps the paper securely fastened (though you can now buy a foil and baking parchment blend that works brilliantly for this and many other purposes). Serve these for an indulgent brunch drizzled with maple syrup and some banana 'yoghurt' (see page 21). You could also serve them as a pudding with a generous scoop of my Vanilla or Strawberry Ice Cream (see pages 205 and 210).

nut free   *gluten free*   *vegan*   *soya free*   *yeast free*

Serves 4
(makes 6–8 pancakes)

300g gluten-free plain flour (ideally Doves Farm)
1 tsp gluten-free baking powder
45g golden caster sugar
A pinch of sea salt flakes
500ml rice milk
60ml sunflower oil, plus extra for frying (optional)
100g apple purée (see the Glossary, page 225)
Maple syrup, for drizzling

For the roasted fruit
700g fresh soft fruit of your choice (such as plums, peaches, nectarines, apricots, bananas, hulled strawberries)
½ tsp ground cinnamon
2 tbsp soft light brown sugar

Preheat the oven to 200°C (400°F), gas mark 6.

First, prepare the fruit, removing any stones and chopping the flesh into bite-sized pieces. Place in the middle of one large piece of baking parchment, sprinkle over the cinnamon and sugar and fold the parchment up to enclose the fruit in a neat parcel. Secure the parcel with string (unless using a parchment and foil blend – see above), then place on a baking tray and bake in the oven for 15–20 minutes.

Meanwhile, sift the flour and baking powder into a large mixing bowl and add the sugar and salt. In a separate bowl, whisk together the rice milk, sunflower oil and apple purée. Pour the liquid ingredients over the flour mixture and whisk until smooth.

Place a medium-sized non-stick frying pan over a medium heat. (You will need a good non-stick pan for this recipe; if you think it may stick in any way, then lightly oil the frying pan before adding the pancake mix.) Spoon a ladleful (around 100ml) of the pancake batter into the hot pan. Cook for 1–2 minutes or until you start to see bubbles rise to the surface and the batter begins to dry and curl at the edges. Carefully flip the pancake over and cook until lightly golden – a further 1–2 minutes.

Continue until you have made all of the pancakes – you can keep them warm in the oven wrapped in foil. Serve with the roasted fruit and a drizzle of maple syrup.

potato
farls

Fluffy, crisp and yet satisfyingly hearty, potato farls make an excellent breakfast dish. I like to serve them with a pile of smoked salmon, some ripe avocado (thinly sliced) and a generous squeeze of lemon juice; it makes a wonderful weekend brunch, especially when accompanied by a glass of fresh orange juice and a rice milk latte. They are a lovely addition to a cooked breakfast, too, served alongside grilled bacon and tomatoes, baked beans and mushrooms – just what you need on a cold wintry morning. Leftover mashed potato works particularly well in this dish, as the mash needs to have cooled down for a few hours first. It's best if no fat is added, though, as it helps the consistency of farls if the potato is as dry as possible.

nut free   gluten free   vegan   soya free   yeast free

Makes 8 potato farls

500g floury potatoes (such as Maris Piper)
125g gluten-free plain flour (ideally Doves Farm), plus extra for dusting
¼ tsp mustard powder (optional)
½ tsp sea salt flakes
1½ tbsp olive oil

Peel the potatoes and cut into 5cm chunks, then place in a saucepan, add a pinch of salt and cover with water. Bring to the boil and then reduce the heat slightly and simmer for 7 minutes or until the potatoes are completely tender to the point of a knife. Drain the potatoes, return them to the pan and mash until smooth, but without adding any fat at this stage. Leave the mash to cool for at least a few hours or even overnight. Alternatively, use the equivalent in weight (about 500g) of leftover mashed potato. (Don't worry if it contains oil or margarine.)

When you are ready to cook the farls, sift the plain flour, mustard powder (if using) and salt into a large bowl. Add 1 tablespoon of the olive oil and the mashed potato and mix together by hand until all the ingredients are fully blended and have been kneaded into a large ball.

Dust a rolling pin and a work surface or large board with flour and then divide the farl mixture into two even-sized balls. Lay them on the work surface and lightly roll each into a circle approximately 19cm in diameter. Using a palette knife, cut each circle into quarters.

Pour the remaining olive oil into a non-stick frying pan set over a medium heat. When the oil is hot, place the farls in the pan (four at a time) and fry for 3 minutes on each side or until crisp and golden. Repeat with the remaining farls (which you can keep hot by wrapping in foil and placing in a warm oven) and then serve.

maple syrup scones

Crumbly, sweet and dense in texture, these scones are just the thing for breakfast, served warm with a pat of dairy-free margarine and a milky coffee. The maple syrup and brown sugar add a mellow flavour of molasses, while the oats give texture and a hearty feel. I recommend eating these fresh on the day that they are baked.

nut free   gluten free   vegan   soya free   yeast free

Makes 8 scones

300g gluten-free self-raising flour (ideally Doves Farm)
1 tsp gluten-free baking powder
75g soft light brown sugar
100g gluten-free porridge oats
A pinch of sea salt flakes
60ml sunflower oil
80ml maple syrup
125ml rice milk
1 tsp vanilla extract

Preheat the oven to 180°C (350°F), gas mark 4, and line a baking sheet with baking parchment.

Sift the flour and baking powder into a large mixing bowl, then add the sugar, oats and salt and stir together. Pour in the sunflower oil, maple syrup, rice milk and vanilla extract and gently fold in using a metal spoon until all the ingredients are combined. The dough will be tacky in consistency and sticky to handle, but you should be able to pull it into a ball before transferring it to the lined baking sheet.

Next, shape the dough into a circle about 18cm in diameter. Take a sharp knife and lightly score the circle into eight wedges, cutting into the dough to a depth of about 1cm.

Bake for 25 minutes or until golden and fragrant, then remove from the oven and, while the scone 'loaf' is still hot, cut into wedges and leave to cool a little before serving warm.

chickpea bread
for toast & jam

This is the perfect bread for toasting for breakfast, though I also enjoy it freshly baked and made into a sandwich. If you've been looking for a loaf that's free from gluten, dairy produce, eggs and yeast, then I cannot recommend this one highly enough. It's a very easy and effective recipe that uses gram flour, which is made from chickpeas, and I hope you'll be delighted with the results. One word of advice, though: once it's out of the oven, leave the bread to cool down completely before cutting into it. If you cut into a loaf made with allergy-friendly ingredients while it's still warm, you'll find the middle is still gummy in texture, but once it has cooled it should form a decent crumb. If stored wrapped in foil in the fridge or in an airtight tin on a countertop, the bread will keep for up to three days; after that it tends to turn very dry and crumbly. It's delicious served lightly toasted and spread with a little dairy-free margarine and some jam of your choice, though slices of avocado sprinkled with sea salt make a wonderful variation, as does a layer of peanut butter and a few sliced tomatoes – the options are many!

nut free   gluten free   vegan   soya free   yeast free

Makes 1 loaf

Sunflower oil, for greasing
350g gluten-free plain flour
    (ideally Doves Farm)
250g gram flour
2 tsp gluten-free baking
    powder
1 tsp bicarbonate of soda
1 tbsp ground flaxseed
½ tsp sea salt flakes
1 tsp cider vinegar

Equipment
You will need a 900g
    (11cm x 22cm) loaf tin
    for this recipe

Preheat the oven to 200°C (400°F), gas mark 6, and generously grease your loaf tin with sunflower oil.

Sift the two flours, baking powder and bicarbonate of soda into a large mixing bowl, add the flaxseed and salt and whisk together until combined. Pour over 435ml of water and the cider vinegar and mix together gently with a wooden spoon until all the ingredients are incorporated. The mixture will be quite loose in consistency – you will be able to form it into a soft ball of dough, but it will be too sticky to handle properly.

Transfer the dough to the loaf tin and level the top with the back of your spoon. Place in the oven and bake for 40 minutes or until risen and golden brown. Remove from the tin and leave to cool completely on a wire rack before slicing.

hot-smoked salmon kedgeree with cashew sauce

This Anglo-Indian dish has long been enjoyed as part of a robust breakfast. The level of spice is usually mild enough to let the smoked fish take the lead, adding a wonderful depth of flavour to the rice. There are countless incarnations of this dish, of course, and while I've specified hot-smoked salmon in this recipe, feel free to swap it for another type of fish: smoked haddock or trout or even prawns would work well. Kedgeree is normally served with poached or soft-boiled eggs on top. Here, I've created a creamy cashew sauce, both as a nod to the richness of the egg yolk and to offset the spices. If you can't eat nuts, then I recommend you serve it with my avocado cream (see page 182) – the fresh taste and rich texture of the avocado really complements the dish. Served for breakfast, lunch or supper, it's delicious at any time of the day.

contains nuts *nut-free option* *gluten free* *dairy free* *egg free* *soya free* *yeast free*

Serves 4

1 large white onion
4 cardamom pods
1 tbsp olive oil
2 heaped tsp mild curry powder
¼ tsp ground cinnamon
¼ tsp turmeric
175g brown basmati rice
500ml vegetable stock (see the Glossary, page 232) or water
300g hot-smoked salmon
A small bunch of flat-leaf parsley
Sea salt flakes and freshly ground black pepper

For the cashew sauce (or serve with the avocado cream on page 182 for a nut-free option)
75g cashew nuts
A good pinch of sea salt flakes

Finely chop the onion and carefully split the cardamom pods open. Place the olive oil in a large saucepan over a medium heat, add the chopped onion and fry gently for 5–8 minutes or until softened but not browned. Add all of the spices, turn up the heat a little and continue to fry for a further 2 minutes.

Stir in the rice, pour over the stock or water, then cover with a lid and bring to the boil. Reduce the heat and simmer gently for 25–30 minutes or until the rice has absorbed all of the liquid.

Meanwhile, flake the hot-smoked salmon (discarding the skin) and finely chop the parsley, then make the cashew sauce (if using).

In a heavy-based frying pan, dry-fry the cashew nuts over a medium–high heat, shaking the pan regularly to stop them catching, for 5–8 minutes or until lightly golden. Transfer the cashews to a mortar, sprinkle over the salt and pour in 6 tablespoons of water. Using the pestle, grind the cashews down into the water until you have a thick and creamy paste, adding a little more water to the mixture if you think it needs it. (Don't be alarmed if it looks as if there is too much liquid to start with; you will find that the more you grind the nuts, the thicker the sauce will become.) Alternatively, place the cashews, salt and water in a high-powered blender and blitz until smooth and creamy, scraping down the sides of the machine when necessary.

Fluff the rice up with a fork and then stir the flaked salmon and chopped parsley into the rice until combined. Season to taste with salt and pepper, then spoon the kedgeree into bowls and drizzle over the cashew sauce or avocado cream to serve.

breakfasts

sunflower seed
butter cookies
chocolate chip biscuits
brown sugar
oat biscuits
lemon loaf cake
oat & stem
ginger cookies
cherry &
almond biscuits
lemon shortbread
spicy cinnamon cookies
mississippi
mud brownies
christmas biscuits
coconut loaf
chocolate
banana bread
strawberry &
cream cupcakes

elevenses

sunflower seed butter cookies

These cookies are a favourite of mine: simple, delicious and perfect for sharing with family and friends. The combination of dark brown sugar and sunflower seed butter gives the biscuits a rich and decadent flavour, reminiscent of the American peanut cookies I remember eating as a child. You can replace the sunflower seed butter with crunchy peanut butter or almond butter, if you prefer – either would work equally well. Enjoy these cookies straight from the oven and treat yourself, as the longer they are kept, the less crisp they will become – all the more reason to help yourself to another one!

nut free   gluten free   vegan   soya free   yeast free

Makes around 16 cookies

90g dairy-free margarine
4 tbsp sunflower seed butter (see the Glossary, pages 232–3)
125g soft dark brown sugar
1 heaped tsp egg replacer (ideally Orgran) whisked with 2 tbsp water
125g gluten-free plain flour (ideally Doves Farm)
½ tsp bicarbonate of soda
A pinch of ground cinnamon

Preheat the oven to 180°C (350°F), gas mark 4, and line two baking sheets with baking parchment.

Place the margarine, sunflower seed butter and sugar in a large mixing bowl and beat together with a wooden spoon until light and creamy. Stir in the egg replacer mixture, a bit at a time, until incorporated. (Don't worry if the mixture splits; adding the flour will bring it back together.) Sift in the flour, bicarbonate of soda and cinnamon and stir together until fully mixed.

Scoop heaped teaspoonfuls of the mixture onto the baking sheets – around eight little 'mounds' on each tray and spaced evenly apart, bearing in mind that they will spread during cooking.

Bake in the oven for 12 minutes or until fragrant and golden, swapping the baking sheets around halfway through cooking. Leave to cool for 5 minutes on the sheets (the cookies will still be very soft at this point and will collapse if you move them too soon) and then transfer to a wire rack to finish cooling.

chocolate
chip biscuits

These lovely biscuits – slightly crisp on the outside and just a little chewy in the centre – are both intolerance friendly and utterly moreish. The mere scent of them baking is irresistible, and they live up to expectations with their intense chocolate flavour – everyone will love them, adults and children alike. Stored in an airtight container, they will keep for two to three days. Alternatively, you can freeze the dough, simply defrosting and then shaping it into cookies when you are ready to bake.

nut free   *gluten free*   *vegan*   *soya free*   *yeast free*

Makes around 32 biscuits

50g dairy- and soya-free dark chocolate
110g dairy-free margarine
55g golden caster sugar
110g soft light brown sugar
220g gluten-free self-raising flour (ideally Doves Farm)
15g cocoa powder
1 tsp gluten-free baking powder
1 tbsp ground flaxseed
A good pinch of sea salt flakes
2 tbsp rice milk

Preheat the oven to 180°C (350°F), gas mark 4, and line two baking sheets with baking parchment.

Roughly chop the chocolate into little pieces and set aside, then place the margarine, caster sugar and brown sugar in a large mixing bowl and cream together using a wooden spoon until incorporated and smooth.

Sift the flour, cocoa powder and baking powder into the bowl, add the ground flaxseed and the salt and mix in until combined – it will look rather clumpy at this stage.

Add the chocolate pieces and rice milk to the cookie mixture and beat together until the dough forms a large ball. (You can at this stage use your hands to pull the mixture together.)

Take a heaped teaspoonful of the dough and roll it into a small ball before pressing it gently with the flat of your hand so that it forms a disc about 4cm in diameter and 5mm thick. Place on one of the lined baking sheets and repeat with the rest of the mixture, spacing the biscuits 3cm or so apart and allowing about eight per sheet.

Place in the oven and bake for 12–15 minutes or until just firm to the touch and slightly cracking on top, swapping the baking sheets around after about 8 minutes. Remove from the oven and leave to cool and firm up for 2 minutes before transferring to a wire rack to cool down fully.

brown sugar
oat biscuits

These delicious oaty biscuits are sweet, malty and crisp but with just the right amount of chew to them. Perfect served as a mid-morning snack, they have more than a passing resemblance to the ever-popular Hobnob, though of course these are completely intolerance friendly! If you keep them in an airtight container, they will last for up to five days, though they do get softer as the days go on.

contains nuts   nut-free option   gluten free   vegan   soya free   yeast free

Makes around 15 biscuits

125g gluten-free plain flour (ideally Doves Farm)
100g gluten-free porridge oats
50g ground almonds (or desiccated coconut for a nut-free option)
100g soft light brown sugar
½ tsp bicarbonate of soda
1 tbsp boiling water
75ml sunflower oil
3 tbsp golden syrup or agave syrup

Preheat the oven to 180°C (350°F), gas mark 4, and line two baking sheets with baking parchment.

Sift the flour into a large bowl and stir in the oats, ground almonds (or desiccated coconut) and brown sugar until evenly mixed.

Place the bicarbonate of soda in a small bowl and add the boiling water, then tip this mixture into the dry ingredients along with the sunflower oil and golden syrup or agave syrup. Tip all of the mixture into a food processor and pulse until starting to pull together. Remove the blade and scoop up a tablespoonful of the biscuit mixture and squeeze it between the palms of your hands so that it binds together – it will still be a little crumbly. Shape into a ball and press flat between your hands until about 1cm thick, then place on one of the baking sheets.

Repeat with the rest of the mixture, spacing the biscuits evenly apart to allow them to spread a little during cooking.

Bake in the oven for 15–18 minutes or until golden brown and fragrant, swapping the baking sheets around after 10 minutes. Remove from the oven and leave for 10 minutes to firm up before transferring to a wire rack to cool down completely.

lemon
loaf cake

This sweet and citrusy loaf is incredibly easy to make but very rewarding for such little effort – the perfect cake to make with children or to whip up quickly if unexpected visitors arrive. It is the ideal accompaniment to a pot of Earl Grey tea, served either in the morning or afternoon. The inclusion of oil and water not only makes preparation very simple, but means that no egg replacer is needed, as the mixture is moist enough to form a light crumb. It also means that the cake won't keep as long, however, as it can dry out and so is best served on the day it's made. All the more reason, I think, to share it out as a family treat!

nut free   gluten free   vegan   soya free   yeast free

Serves 8

275g gluten-free plain flour (ideally Doves Farm)
1 tsp gluten-free baking powder
200g golden caster sugar
Grated zest and juice of 1 lemon
100ml sunflower or rapeseed oil, plus extra for greasing

For the icing
100g icing sugar
2 tbsp lemon juice

Equipment
You will need a 900g (11cm x 22cm) loaf tin for this recipe

Preheat the oven to 200°C (400°F), gas mark 6, then lightly grease the loaf tin with sunflower or rapeseed oil and line it with baking parchment.

Sift the flour and baking powder into a large mixing bowl, then stir in the sugar and lemon zest. Pour over the lemon juice, sunflower or rapeseed oil and 170ml of water and mix together until smooth and glossy.

Pour into the prepared loaf tin and bake in the oven for 30 minutes or until golden and slightly risen. Remove from the oven and leave to cool in the tin while you make the icing.

Sift the icing sugar into a bowl, add the lemon juice and mix together until smooth and creamy. Once the lemon loaf is completely cool, remove from the tin, spread over the icing and leave to set for 30 minutes before cutting into slices to serve.

oat & stem ginger cookies

These cookies are wonderfully chewy, with just enough bite to make them a satisfying eat. Stem ginger is a particular favourite of mine and adds a lovely flavour and texture to the cookies. They are delicious served while still warm, accompanied by a cup of tea. Equally, they will keep for up to two days if stored in an airtight container.

nut free   gluten free   vegan   soya free   yeast free

Makes about 21 cookies

150g gluten-free porridge oats
100g preserved stem ginger (about 5 balls)
150g gluten-free plain flour (ideally Doves Farm)
1 tsp bicarbonate of soda
1 tsp ground ginger
1½ tsp xanthan gum
150g soft light brown sugar
50g ground flaxseed
100g apple purée (see the Glossary, page 225)
150ml rapeseed oil

Preheat the oven to 170°C (325°F), gas mark 3, and line two baking sheets with baking parchment.

Place the oats in a food processor and pulse until finely ground and then finely chop the stem ginger. Next, sift the flour, bicarbonate of soda, ground ginger and xanthan gum into a large mixing bowl and add the ground oats, sugar and ground flaxseed, then whisk together until combined.

Add the apple purée and rapeseed oil to the dry ingredients and stir together until mixed and coming together into a dough. Finally, stir in the chopped ginger until evenly distributed.

Scoop up a heaped tablespoon of the mixture and shape into a ball. Place on one of the baking sheets and carefully flatten into a disc approximately 5cm in diameter. Repeat with the rest of the mixture, allowing about ten cookies per baking sheet and leaving at least 3cm between each one, as they will spread a little while baking.

Bake in the oven for 17–20 minutes or until fragrant and golden, swapping the baking sheets around after about 10 minutes. Leave to cool a little on the baking sheets and then transfer to a wire rack to cool down completely.

contains
nuts

cherry &
almond biscuits

Shortbread–like in consistency, enriched with ground almonds and studded with sweet cherry 'jewels', these little treats were first made for me by a friend. They have a wonderfully addictive almond flavour, which I've enhanced in my version of the recipe by using almond extract – selecting the natural extract over the synthetic almond essence tastes so much better, in my opinion. As a small word of warning, please note that it's best to err on the side of caution with your baking times and to keep an eye on your biscuits as they bake. If you cook them for too long, they can become a little too crisp and shatter when you bite into them – not what you want at all.

contains nuts   gluten free   vegan   soya free   yeast free

Makes about 15 biscuits

80g glacé cherries
115g dairy-free margarine
60g golden caster sugar
180g gluten-free plain flour
    (ideally Doves Farm)
60g ground almonds
1 tbsp almond extract

Equipment
You will need a 6cm round
    pastry cutter for this
    recipe

Preheat the oven to 170°C (325°F), gas mark 3, and line two baking sheets with baking parchment.

Begin by chopping up the cherries. Using a wooden spoon, cream together the margarine and the sugar in a large mixing bowl until light and fluffy. Sift in the flour, then add the ground almonds, almond extract and chopped cherries and stir everything together until the mixture forms a buttery dough – you may need to pull it together a little with your hands.

Shape the biscuit dough into a large ball and place between two sheets of cling film. Roll out the dough to about 5mm thick – any thinner and the dough will be difficult to handle. Remove the topmost layer of cling film and use the pastry cutter to cut out the biscuits. Cut out as many as possible from your layer of dough, then roll up the remaining dough into a ball and use the same method to roll it out before cutting out the remaining biscuits.

Place on the lined baking sheets and bake in the oven for about 15 minutes or until fragrant and golden, swapping the baking sheets around after about 8 minutes. Remove from the oven and transfer to a wire rack to cool.

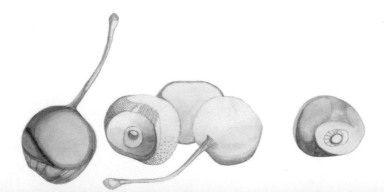

elevenses

elevenses

lemon
shortbread

All shortbread, whatever its flavour, demands a crisp and crumbly texture that collapses delightfully as you bite into it. This lemon shortbread doesn't disappoint and is so wonderfully easy to prepare. Within a short space of time, you will have delicious biscuits to offer friends and family. Ground rice (different from rice flour – see the Glossary, pages 228 and 232) is white rice that has been coarsely ground; it is perfect for using in intolerance-friendly cakes and puddings to help give a light and fluffy texture. Once baked, the shortbread will keep for two to three days if stored in an airtight container.

nut free   gluten free   vegan   soya free   yeast free

Makes about 15 biscuits

100g dairy-free margarine
50g golden caster sugar
Grated zest of 1 lemon
150g gluten-free plain flour
    (ideally Doves Farm), plus
    extra for dusting
50g ground rice
2 tbsp demerara sugar

Preheat the oven to 190°C (375°F), gas mark 5, and line two baking sheets with baking parchment,

Place the margarine and sugar in a large mixing bowl and cream together with a wooden spoon until light and fluffy. Stir in the lemon zest, then sift in the flour, add the ground rice and stir together until the mixture begins to form a dough.

Using your hands, knead the dough until combined and smooth. Transfer to a work surface or wooden board lightly dusted in flour and roll the biscuit dough into a thick sausage shape approximately 18cm long and 7cm wide.

Sprinkle the work surface or board with the demerara sugar and then roll the biscuit dough in it until well coated. Cut into 15 rounds (they will be about 1cm thick) and then lay them flat on the lined baking sheets. Bake in the oven for 18–20 minutes or until fragrant and lightly golden, swapping the baking sheets around after about 10 minutes. Remove from the oven and transfer to a wire rack to cool before serving.

spicy
cinnamon cookies

Sweet, spicy and completely moreish, these cookies have such an intense flavour – thanks, in part, to the addition of apple purée and copious amounts of cinnamon and ginger. The apple purée also means that there is no call for eggs or indeed much fat, making them a healthier alternative to your average cookie. They are incredibly simple to make and hence perfect for baking with children – stirring being the only real necessity. I recommend serving them still warm from the oven, or certainly on the day that they are made; they will keep for a few more days but will get softer as time goes on. That said, if you pop them in a hot oven (preheated to 180°C/350°F/gas mark 4) and re-bake them for 3–5 minutes, they will crisp up and become chewy again – not to mention warm. Delicious!

nut free   gluten free   vegan   soya free   yeast free

Makes about 20 cookies

250g gluten-free self-raising flour (ideally Doves Farm)
1 tsp bicarbonate of soda
2 tsp ground cinnamon
1 tsp ground ginger
½ tsp ground mixed spice
150g soft dark brown sugar
100g apple purée (see the Glossary, page 225)
4 tbsp golden syrup or agave syrup
2 tbsp sunflower or rapeseed oil

Preheat the oven to 180°C (350°F), gas mark 4, and line two baking sheets with baking parchment.

Sift the flour, bicarbonate of soda and spices into a bowl. Place the sugar, apple purée, golden syrup and sunflower or rapeseed oil in a large mixing bowl and beat together for 2–3 minutes or until smooth and glossy.

Add the dry ingredients a little at a time, stirring as you go, until they are fully incorporated and you have a thick but loose and slightly sticky cookie dough.

Use a tablespoon to scoop up a ball of dough and then place on one of the lined baking sheets. Repeat with the remaining mixture, placing the cookies on the baking sheets and leaving a few centimetres between each cookie, as they will spread out slightly while cooking.

Bake in the oven for about 15 minutes or until set and fragrant, swapping the baking sheets around after about 8 minutes, then leave to cool for 5 minutes before transferring to a wire rack to cool down fully. Eat immediately or store in an airtight container for up to two days.

mississippi mud brownies

I've named this recipe after Mississippi mud pie, so called for its resemblance to the rich, muddy banks of the Mississippi River. The beauty of these brownies is that they have all the density of the original, yet contain very little fat or sugar – and they are, of course, completely allergen free. Dates, cooked down to a gloriously gooey purée, make up the body and sweetness of the brownies, while ground flaxseed helps bind the mixture and adds nutrients, too. Serve them warm from the oven or cold with a cup of coffee. They're also delicious served as a pudding, a generous pouring of custard or a dollop of my Vanilla or Chocolate Ice Cream (see pages 213, 205 and 211) transforming them into a decadent treat.

nut free   gluten free   vegan   soya free   yeast free

Makes 12 brownies

200g dried dates
200g pitted dates
½ tsp bicarbonate of soda
225g gluten-free plain flour
  (ideally Doves Farm)
25g cocoa powder
1 tsp gluten-free baking
  powder
65g ground flaxseed
150g soft dark brown sugar
150g dairy- and soya-free
  dark chocolate
250ml rice milk

Equipment
You will need a 20cm square
  baking tin for this recipe

Preheat the oven to 170°C (325°F), gas mark 3, and line the baking tin with baking parchment.

Roughly chop the dates and place in a saucepan with 250ml of water and the bicarbonate of soda. Bring to a gentle simmer and cook for 15 minutes over a low–medium heat, stirring regularly, until the dates have formed a soft and thick purée. Remove from the heat and set aside to cool down.

Sift the flour, cocoa powder and baking powder into a large mixing bowl and add the ground flaxseed and brown sugar, then stir together until evenly mixed.

Break the chocolate into small chunks and place in a bowl set over a saucepan filled to a depth of 2–3cm with boiling water. Set the pan over a low heat and allow the chocolate to melt until smooth.

Add the melted chocolate, date purée and rice milk to the dry ingredients and fold in until evenly incorporated and forming a smooth batter. Pour the mixture into the baking tin and bake in the oven for 30–35 minutes or until lightly risen. (The sponge should be a little bit gooey in the middle. You can test it with a cocktail stick or skewer: if a little of the uncooked mixture still clings to the stick or skewer when you remove it, then the brownies will be perfectly cooked.) Remove from the oven and leave to cool in the tin before dividing the cake into portions to serve.

christmas biscuits

If I were to choose my favourite time of year, Christmas would undoubtedly be it: the festive lights and decorations, the abundance and richness of the food and the pleasure of giving (and indeed receiving!) always fill me with good cheer. I think it's important to have a few easy tricks up your sleeve for this time of year, and a stock of homemade biscuits and perhaps a Gingerbread Loaf (see page 106) to serve to guests (unexpected or otherwise) will certainly help. These biscuits are so easy to run up and can be cut out and decorated in any way you wish. They'd make a rather lovely Christmas gift, too – presented in a pretty tin with a ribbon tied around it. Once made, they will keep for up to five days in an airtight container.

contains nuts   nut-free option   gluten free   vegan   soya free   yeast free

Makes about 20 round biscuits

60g dairy-free margarine
110g golden caster sugar
175g gluten-free plain flour
    (ideally Doves Farm)
2 tsp ground cinnamon
1 tsp ground ginger
60g ground almonds (or
    ground rice for a
    nut-free option)
1 tbsp vanilla extract

For the icing
150g icing sugar
2–3 tbsp rice milk

To decorate (optional)
1 ball of preserved stem
    ginger, finely chopped
Sprinkles

Equipment
You will need a 6cm round
    pastry cutter or any other
    cutter of your choice for
    this recipe

Preheat the oven to 170°C (325°F), gas mark 3, and line two baking sheets with baking parchment.

Begin by creaming together the margarine and the sugar in a large mixing bowl using a wooden spoon until light and fluffy. Sift in the flour and spices and add the ground almonds (or ground rice, if using) and vanilla extract, then stir together until the mixture forms a buttery dough – you may need to pull it together a little with your hands.

Shape the dough into a large ball and place between two sheets of cling film. Roll out the dough to about 5mm thick – any thinner and the dough will be difficult to handle. Remove the topmost layer of cling film and use your chosen cutter to cut out the biscuits. Cut out as many as possible from your layer of dough, then roll up the remaining dough and use the same method to roll it out before cutting out more biscuits.

Place on the lined baking sheets and bake in the oven for about 15 minutes or until fragrant and golden, swapping the baking sheets around after about 8 minutes. Remove from the oven and transfer to a wire rack to cool.

While the biscuits are cooling, make the icing. Sift the icing sugar into a mixing bowl and then pour in the rice milk, stirring as you go until you have a smooth and spreadable icing. Ice the biscuits, then decorate with chopped stem ginger or sprinkles (if using) and leave the icing to set before serving.

coconut
loaf

Coconut loaf, like my Chocolate Banana Bread or Lemon Loaf Cake (see pages 46 and 36), sits somewhere between cake and bread, making it perfect either as a snack or for breakfast. It's also really simple to put together, and tastes delicious straight from the oven, which means it's the ideal cake to knock up for unexpected guests, or if you simply have the urge to bake. What's more, using only store-cupboard ingredients, it can be made at any time of year. Coconut loaf tastes wonderful spread with my Lemon Curd (see page 97), and I have it on good authority that a slice of this cake and a mug of hot chocolate can soothe many a woe.

nut free   *gluten free*   *vegan*   *soya free*   *yeast free*

Serves 8

300g gluten-free plain flour (ideally Doves Farm)
2 tsp gluten-free baking powder
1 tsp ground cinnamon
4 tbsp ground flaxseed
225g golden caster sugar
150g desiccated coconut
350ml rice milk
50ml sunflower oil, plus extra for greasing

Equipment
You will need a 900g (11cm x 22cm) loaf tin for this recipe

Preheat the oven to 180°C (350°F), gas mark 4, and lightly grease the loaf tin with sunflower oil.

Sift the flour, baking powder and cinnamon into a large mixing bowl, add the ground flaxseed, caster sugar and desiccated coconut and whisk together until evenly combined. Pour over the rice milk and sunflower oil and stir together until you have a thick batter.

Tip the batter into the prepared tin and bake in the oven for 45–50 minutes or until the loaf has risen slightly and is golden brown on top.

Leave to cool in the tin for a few minutes and then turn out onto a wire rack to cool down fully. Serve warm or cold, depending on your mood. If stored in an airtight container, the loaf will keep for up to three days.

chocolate banana bread

Delicious and easy to make, banana bread is always popular in my house, but this recipe is a cut above. The addition of cocoa powder and soft brown sugar, with its mellow caramel flavour, transforms the loaf into something much richer and more elegant. I would go as far as to say that you could serve this bread as a pudding; it's just right for a relaxed supper party with friends, sliced warm from the oven with a scoop of my Vanilla Ice Cream (see page 205) on the side. Really, though, it is wonderful at any time of day, and such a breeze to make, as you simply combine everything in a food processor and then let the oven do the work – bliss!

nut free   *gluten free*   *vegan*   *soya free*   *yeast free*

Serves 8

4 tbsp ground flaxseed
¼ tsp gluten-free baking
   powder
225g gluten-free plain flour
   (ideally Doves Farm)
1 tsp bicarbonate of soda
2 tbsp cocoa powder
100g soft light brown sugar
2 large ripe bananas
125ml sunflower or
   rapeseed oil

Equipment
You will need a 900g
   (11cm x 22cm) loaf tin
   for this recipe

Preheat the oven to 200°C (400°F), gas mark 6, and line the loaf tin with baking parchment.

Place the ground flaxseed and baking powder in a small bowl with 6 tablespoons of water, then stir together and set aside to thicken up. Sift the flour, bicarbonate of soda and cocoa powder into the bowl of a food processor and add the sugar. Break up the bananas into chunks and add them to the dry ingredients.

Pour over the sunflower or rapeseed oil and add the flaxseed mixture, then blitz in the food processor into a smooth and glossy batter.

Pour the batter into the prepared loaf tin and smooth the top with the back of a spoon. Bake in the oven for 25–30 minutes or until slightly risen and fragrant. Leave to rest in the tin for a few minutes before transferring to a wire rack to cool. Cut into slices and serve either warm or cold. The loaf will keep for up to three days in an airtight container.

strawberry & cream cupcakes

Life is dotted with special occasions, and we take so many of them for granted. Yet these moments, however cyclical, all build to leave us with rich memories. Childhood treats, in particular, take on almost mystical qualities when seen through the fog of adulthood. These cupcakes offer an allergen-free take on those little treats one devoured as a child. I love the idea of using fruit to help bind and add an extra layer of flavour, and these little cakes are very fruity indeed! Raspberries would work just as well as strawberries. Topped with a generous layer of vanilla buttercream icing, they're perfect as a special mid-morning or mid-afternoon snack, whether for a celebration with friends or a children's tea party.

nut free   gluten free   vegan   soya free   yeast free

Makes 12 cupcakes

200g fresh strawberries, plus
  a few extra to decorate
4 tbsp ground flaxseed
100ml sunflower oil
100g golden caster sugar
180g gluten-free self-raising
  flour (ideally Doves Farm)
1 tsp bicarbonate of soda

For the vanilla
buttercream icing
55g dairy-free margarine
30ml rice milk or other dairy-
  free milk of your choice
½ tsp vanilla extract
250g golden icing sugar

Equipment
You will need a 12-hole muffin
  or cupcake tin for this
  recipe

Preheat the oven to 180°C (350°F), gas mark 4, and line the muffin or cupcake tin with paper cases.

Hull the strawberries and place in a mixing bowl. Use a fork to mash them until pulpy and juicy. Place the ground flaxseed in a small bowl with 6 tablespoons of water, then stir together and set aside to thicken up.

Pour the sunflower oil into a large mixing bowl, add the sugar and beat together until combined. Stir in the flaxseed and water mixture until incorporated (it will be slightly tacky in consistency). Add the mashed strawberries, then sift in the flour and bicarbonate of soda and use a metal spoon to fold them into the mixture.

Divide the mixture evenly between the cupcake cases, level the tops and bake in the oven for about 20 minutes or until fragrant and springy to the touch. Remove from the oven and transfer to a wire rack to cool down completely.

Meanwhile, make the buttercream icing. Place the margarine, rice or other milk and vanilla extract in a mixing bowl, sift over half of the icing sugar and whisk all the ingredients together. (This can be done by hand but I recommend using an electric whisk, as it takes some time to get the icing mixture to the right creamy consistency – about 4 minutes in total.) Sift in the remaining icing sugar and continue to whisk until thick and glossy. Place the icing in the fridge until you are ready to spread it over the cupcakes, as it may separate if it gets too warm.

Once the cupcakes are completely cool, spread liberally with the icing and decorate with the fresh strawberries. These little cakes are best eaten on the day they're made, though they will keep for up to two days if stored in the fridge.

chicken schnitzel
with salsa verde
watercress & radish
salad with avocado dressing
king prawn gazpacho
garlic & herb
cashew cream cheese
peperonata,
pea & olive pasta
chicken roasted with
courgette & herb cheese stuffing
caramelised onion tart
lemon & oregano
lamb kebabs
quinoa tabbouleh
grilled chermoula chicken
with avocado quinoa salad
carrot & orange salad
chicken, roasted
tomato & caper herb salad
roasted vegetable socca

al fresco

chicken schnitzel
with salsa verde

As popular with children as it is with adults, chicken schnitzel is very straightforward to prepare and the perfect dish for a casual supper with friends. The crisp polenta crumb is infused with a little smoky paprika, while the tangy salsa verde provides a delightful foil for the chicken. There are all sorts of ways to serve this: I rather like it with steamed basmati rice and a tomato salad, but it would go equally well with mashed potato and some wilted greens or purple-sprouting broccoli; it's even delicious served cold in a wrap with salad and avocado – you can adapt it to suit the season.

nut free   gluten free   dairy free   egg free   soya free   yeast free

Serves 4

4 skinless chicken breasts
1 tsp smoked paprika
120g polenta
60g gram or rice flour
2 tsp cornflour mixed with 6 tbsp rice milk
100ml sunflower oil
Sea salt flakes and freshly ground black pepper

For the salsa verde
A large bunch of flat-leaf parsley
A small bunch of coriander
A small bunch of chives
A small bunch of marjoram
3 tbsp capers, drained and rinsed
Grated zest and juice of ½ lemon
6 tbsp extra-virgin olive oil

Lay each chicken breast between two layers of cling film, then use a meat mallet or rolling pin to lightly flatten the chicken until it is about 1.5cm thick. Once flattened, cut each chicken breast in half.

Mix the smoked paprika with the polenta, then season well with salt and pepper. Next, take three large plates and scatter the gram or rice flour over one of them, pour the cornflour mixture over the second plate and scatter the seasoned polenta over the third.

Now make the salsa verde. Place all the ingredients in a food processor, season well with salt and pepper and blitz very briefly so that you are left with a coarse-textured salsa. Alternatively, chop the herbs and capers roughly by hand and mix with the remaining ingredients. Cover the salsa and chill in the fridge until ready to use.

Take each chicken breast and roll it in the gram or rice flour, then dip it into the cornflour before coating in the polenta mixture. Continue until all the chicken breasts are coated and then repeat the process for each one – topping up the plates with more polenta, flour or cornflour mixture if necessary. Twice dipping creates a nice crisp crust.

Pour the sunflower oil into a heavy-based non-stick frying pan set over a medium heat. When the oil is hot, place the coated chicken breasts in the pan and cook for 3–5 minutes on each side or until the schnitzels are cooked through and golden. I would do this in two batches, depending on the size of your pan; if you try to squeeze too many pieces into the pan at once, the chicken will never brown. Keep the cooked schnitzels warm in the oven while you fry the remaining chicken.

Once all the schnitzels are cooked, serve with the salsa verde spooned on the side.

watercress & radish
salad with avocado dressing

Watercress and radishes start to come into their own once spring has sprung. Their peppery heat warms the palate while their fresh taste and invigorating crunch hint at summer days to come. Packed full of flavour, the avocado dressing not only balances the fieriness of the salad ingredients, but also adds a rich and creamy texture. This salad would go beautifully with a seared steak or meaty field mushrooms. The dressing alone works wonderfully with cold chicken or fish, and would make a quick and simple dip for bread, crudités or even prawns. One word of advice: this salad is best served as soon as it is made, otherwise the dressing can start to discolour slightly.

nut free   gluten free   vegan   soya free   yeast free

Serves 4

10cm piece of cucumber
8–10 radishes
250g watercress

For the avocado dressing
1 ripe Hass avocado
3 tbsp extra-virgin olive oil
2 tbsp lemon juice
1 tsp runny honey or agave
    syrup
Sea salt flakes and freshly
    ground black pepper

First, make the dressing. Scoop out the flesh of the avocado and place in a food processor with the olive oil, lemon juice and honey or agave syrup. Blitz until completely smooth and glossy, then season with salt and pepper to taste.

Peel the cucumber and slice in half lengthways, then cut into thin half-moons. Trim the ends from the radishes and slice into thin rounds. Remove any of the woodier stalks from the watercress and then place in a large serving bowl with the cucumber and radishes and mix everything together. You can then spoon over the dressing and toss to make a very rich salad or serve it in generous dollops on the side.

*Always use ripe Hass avocados to make the dressing
- it is they that give the mixture its
gorgeous velvetiness...*

king prawn gazpacho

Gazpacho may seem a quintessentially summer dish, but once you've tried this version of the classic soup you may be tempted to serve it all year round! Sweet and slightly sour (from the dates, tomatoes and citrus juices), with a delicious mix of creaminess and crunch, this is one of those dishes that not only tastes fabulous but feels as if it's doing you good, too. The idea came from my friend Jo, a very talented raw-food writer and chef. I have tinkered with her original recipe a little, adding the king prawns and avocado to create a sumptuous meal in a bowl – a sort of chilled prawn bouillabaisse, you might say. If you can, use a mixture of tomatoes, both in colour (yellow, red) and type (plum, cherry, heirloom). It just looks so beautiful in the bowl. But if you can only get standard tomatoes, then I recommend going for a mix of large and cherry – all on the vine for added flavour. Rather than using standard dates, you can substitute with Medjool instead, which are much softer and therefore don't need soaking. They are also larger, so you'll need only two dates instead of four. Serve the finished soup with my Chickpea Bread (see page 28) for a delicious and hearty combination.

nut free   *gluten free*   *dairy free*   *egg free*   *soya free*   *yeast free*

Serves 4

4 pitted dates
500g tomatoes (about 6 large or 12 regular-sized tomatoes)
Juice of 1 orange
Juice of 1 lemon
Juice of 1 lime
1 clove of garlic
1 tsp ground cumin
A small pinch of chilli powder
2 tbsp good-quality extra-virgin olive oil, plus extra for drizzling
A small bunch of parsley
A small bunch of coriander
1 small cucumber
1 small red onion
1 large ripe avocado (preferably Hass)
350g cooked and peeled king prawns
Sea salt flakes and freshly ground black pepper

Put the dates in a small bowl, pour over a little boiling water (just enough to cover) and leave to soak for 1 hour.

Place the soaked dates in a blender and add half of the tomatoes (reserving the prettier ones to chop up later), along with the juice of the orange, lemon and lime, the garlic, cumin, chilli powder and olive oil. Blitz until completely smooth and then add the fresh herbs and pulse very briefly until just incorporated. (If you blend the herbs for too long, the gazpacho will turn brown instead of a rich red colour.)

Finely dice the cucumber, onion and remaining tomatoes. Slice the avocado in half, remove the stone and cut the flesh into small chunks before scooping out. Place all of the chopped ingredients in a large mixing bowl and then pour the blended mixture over the top.

Stir in the king prawns and season with salt and pepper to taste. Cover the bowl with cling film and refrigerate the soup for at least an hour before serving. If you make it a day ahead and leave it in the fridge overnight, you'll find that the flavours really develop.

To serve, pour the gazpacho into individual bowls and top with a drizzle of olive oil.

garlic & herb cashew cream cheese

contains nuts

Based on the vegan technique of softening and blending cashew nuts until smooth and creamy, this makes an excellent dairy-free substitute for cream cheese. It's really versatile, too – you can use it in so many different ways: as a dip, for instance, or spread on toast for a light lunch or snack, with a little smoked salmon or sliced tomato on top; stirred into freshly made risotto or folded into pasta with a few peas and some crispy pancetta; or cooked in various dishes, such as my Chicken Ballotine with Courgette and Herb Cheese, Baby Squash with Leeks and Garlic and Herb Cheese or Caramelised Onion Tart (see pages 59, 164 and 61) – the options are endless. Once made, store in a sealed tub in the fridge. Kept like this, it will last for up to five days – just give it a stir before using.

contains nuts   gluten free   vegan   soya free   yeast free

Makes about 650g

300g raw cashew nuts
½ tsp sea salt flakes
160ml vegetable stock (see the Glossary, page 232)
A small bunch of flat-leaf parsley
A small bunch of chives
Leaves from 4–5 sprigs of thyme
1 tbsp lemon juice
1 tbsp garlic oil
Freshly ground black pepper

Place the cashew nuts in a large bowl of water and leave to soak for 6 hours or more. (You can leave the nuts to soak overnight, but I wouldn't recommend any longer than 24 hours.) This softens them, making for a creamier 'cheese'.

Drain the nuts and place in a food processor or high-powered blender. Add the salt and then pour in the stock, bit by bit, as you blitz the mixture, stopping to stir it every now and then, until smooth, thick and creamy – this can take up to 10 minutes. If you taste the 'cheese' and think it seems a little grainy, continue to blitz the mixture, pulsing and stirring as you go and adding a drop more stock if you think it needs it, until completely smooth.

Finely chop the fresh herbs, then add to the mixture with the lemon juice and garlic oil. Season well with pepper and extra salt if needed and pulse until combined. Transfer to a bowl, then cover and chill in the fridge for an hour before using.

al fresco

peperonata, pea & olive pasta

This is a wonderfully light and zingy pasta dish, full of vibrant colour from the peppers, peas and cherry tomatoes. The black olives give a savoury note, while the fresh herbs add extra aroma. A delicious summertime supper, it's incredibly simple to put together, too. Don't be put off by the inclusion of the raw onion and garlic; marinating them in the oil and lemon juice takes away any bitterness, leaving just a slight sharpness that offsets the other flavours.

contains nuts   nut-free option   gluten free   vegan   soya free   yeast free

Serves 4

Juice of ½ lemon
1 small white onion
1 clove of garlic
3 tbsp extra-virgin olive oil, plus extra for coating the peppers
A handful of pine nuts (or omit for a nut-free option)
100g frozen peas
3 peppers (preferably orange, yellow and red)
12 cherry tomatoes
20 pitted black olives
400g gluten-free penne or conchiglie pasta
Leaves from a small bunch of basil
Leaves from a small bunch of flat-leaf parsley
Sea salt flakes and freshly ground black pepper

Preheat the oven to 220°C (425°F), gas mark 7.

Place the lemon juice and a pinch of sea salt in a mixing bowl. Halve the onion and slice into very fine half-moons, then slice the garlic into thin rounds and add them both to the lemon juice. Using your hands, rub the lemon juice into the sliced onion and garlic. Pour in the olive oil, then stir everything together and set aside to marinate while you prepare the rest of the dish.

Place the pine nuts (if using) on a baking sheet and toast in the oven for 3–4 minutes or until golden – be careful not to let them burn as the oven will be very hot for roasting the peppers. Remove from the oven and set aside to cool. Place the frozen peas in a bowl and cover with boiling water. Leave to sit for 5 minutes and then drain in a colander and set aside.

Rub a little olive oil over each pepper, then place on a baking sheet and roast in the oven for 35 minutes or until softened and slightly charred on the outside. Remove from the oven and place in a plastic freezer or storage bag. Seal and leave for around 30 minutes, then take out of the bag and carefully peel off the skin from each pepper, cut out the stalk and remove the seeds.

Next, slice the peppers lengthways into narrow strips and add them to the marinating onion. Slice the cherry tomatoes into halves and stir them and the black olives in with the peppers.

Bring a large saucepan of salted water to the boil, add the pasta and cook until al dente, following the instructions on the packet – usually 10–12 minutes, depending on the brand. Drain in a colander and tip into a large serving bowl. Pour over the peperonata and olive mixture and add the peas. Tear the herb leaves into small pieces, add to the pasta and scatter over the toasted pine nuts (if using). Toss all the ingredients together, seasoning to taste with salt and pepper, and serve while warm.

al fresco

al fresco

chicken ballotine with courgette & herb cheese stuffing

A 'ballotine' is chicken, or other meat, that has been boned and then stuffed before being roasted. This particular recipe, with its rich stuffing, makes a lovely summery dish – perfect for serving to friends and family on a warm day. Because you serve it cold, there's the added benefit of being able to make this the day before, allowing it to develop in flavour. This makes it ideal for a lunch party, especially if accompanied by a selection of salads, baked sweet potatoes and perhaps my Caramelised Onion Tart (see page 61) for a proper feast. On less formal occasions, I like to slice the chicken into 2cm-thick wedges and serve it with a green bean and tomato salad, with a few olives scattered over and some boiled new potatoes – it's a real treat. You can bone the chicken yourself if you know how. If not, simply ask your butcher to do it for you – given a bit of notice, he should be happy to oblige.

contains nuts   *gluten free*   *dairy free*   *egg free*   *soya free*   *yeast free*

Serves 8

450g courgettes
120g pine nuts
1 small white onion
1 tbsp olive oil
60g cooked rice
150g Garlic and Herb Cashew
    Cream Cheese (just over
    a fifth of the full recipe –
    see page 56)
Leaves from a small bunch
    of basil
1 x 1.75–2kg boned chicken
Sea salt flakes and freshly
    ground black pepper

Trim the courgettes and roughly grate them, then place in a large sieve set over a saucepan or bowl and scatter over some sea salt. Cover with a small plate, place a heavy weight on top (a tin of beans would do) and leave to drain for 1 hour before transferring to a clean tea towel and squeezing out any excess water.

Preheat the oven to 180°C (350°F), gas mark 4.

Place the pine nuts on a baking sheet and toast in the oven, turning occasionally to ensure they don't burn, for 5–6 minutes or until golden. Remove from the oven and set aside to cool.

Finely chop the onion, then heat the olive oil in a saucepan, add the onion and soften over a low heat for about 10 minutes or until translucent but not browned. Add the courgettes and continue to fry for a further 5 minutes, stirring every now and then. Remove from the heat and leave to cool down.

Place the courgette and onion mixture in a large mixing bowl and add the cooked rice, toasted pine nuts and cashew cream cheese. Tear up the basil leaves and add them to the mixture, season well with salt and pepper and then mix together with a wooden spoon until combined.

continues...

chicken ballotine with courgette & herb cheese stuffing

Lay the chicken on a chopping board, skin-side down. Spoon the stuffing into the centre of the chicken, then bring the sides of the bird up over the stuffing so they encase it, the edges overlapping slightly. Use cocktail sticks to secure everything together, making a tight 'barrel'. Truss the chicken with butcher's string, then turn it over, stick-side down, and place in a roasting tin.

Roast in the oven for 1¼–1½ hours, then remove, transfer to a plate and cover with foil. Leave to cool for 2–24 hours, keeping it stored in the fridge and removing it 30 minutes or so before serving to allow it to come up to room temperature.

contains
nuts

caramelised
onion tart

A creamy, rich tart may seem out of the question when you're on a diet that's egg, dairy, soy and gluten free. You'll be delighted with this intolerance-friendly version, though, I promise you. Softened, sweet onions and punchy English mustard are combined with my Garlic and Herb Cashew Cream Cheese (see page 56) and used to fill a gluten-free shortcrust pastry case. The result is a delicate but intensely flavoured tart with a soft set centre and a crisp, buttery base. Served warm or at room temperature with a selection of salads, it's perfect for lunch, supper or a picnic feast.

contains nuts   gluten free   vegan   soya free   yeast free

Serves 8

For the shortcrust pastry
230g gluten-free plain flour
  (ideally Doves Farm)
½ tsp xanthan gum
60g vegetable shortening
60g dairy-free margarine
A good pinch of sea salt
  flakes

For the filling
6 white onions
2 tbsp olive oil
3 heaped tsp egg replacer
  (ideally Orgran) whisked
  with 6 tbsp rice milk
200g Garlic and Herb
  Cashew Cream Cheese
  (just over a third of the full
  recipe – see page 56)
1 tsp English mustard
  (1 heaped tsp mustard
  powder mixed with 1 tsp
  water) or homemade
  mustard (see the Glossary,
  page 229)
Sea salt flakes and freshly
  ground black pepper

Equipment
You will need a 23cm round
  tart tin with a removable
  base for this recipe

Begin by cooking the onions for the filling. Halve the onions and then slice into thin half-moons approximately 3mm thick. Heat the olive oil in a large heavy-based saucepan and cook the onions over a low heat until softened and translucent but not browned – this will take about 35 minutes. Once cooked, remove from the heat and leave to cool down.

Meanwhile, preheat the oven to 200°C (400°F), gas mark 6, and place a large baking sheet inside to heat up.

To make the pastry, sift the flour and xanthan gum into the bowl of a food processor. Cut the vegetable shortening into cubes and add to the flour with the margarine and salt, then pulse until the mixture is of a breadcrumb-like consistency. Alternatively, place the ingredients in a large mixing bowl and rub together with your fingertips.

Add 2 tablespoons of cold water, pulsing as you go (or stirring with a flat-bladed knife if making the pastry by hand), until the mixture begins to pull together to form a dough. Add another tablespoon of water if you think it needs it.

Tip the pastry into a large bowl (or keep in the same bowl, if making it by hand) and, using your fingertips, pull together into a ball. Knead lightly for about 2 minutes or until smooth and elastic to your touch.

continues...

al fresco

caramelised
onion tart

Shape the pastry into a ball and place between two large sheets of cling film, then roll it out into a circle slightly larger than the tart tin and no thinner than 3mm.

Peel off the uppermost sheet of cling film and carefully turn the pastry into the tin. Peel away the remaining cling film and gently press the pastry into the sides of the tin, filling in any cracks or gaps with extra pastry patted flat with your fingertips. Trim the edges and set aside while you continue preparing the filling.

Season the egg replacer mixture well with salt and pepper and stir in the cashew cream cheese, mustard and softened onions. Pour the filling into the pastry case and place in the oven on the preheated baking sheet. Bake for 45 minutes or until just set and golden on top. Remove from the oven and leave in the tin for 20 minutes before serving warm or transfer to a wire rack to cool down completely.

If you want to play with the flavours here you can also add ingredients to the caramelised onion mixture: cooked, crispy smoked bacon, chopped chestnuts and sundried tomatoes are all delicious additions...

lemon & oregano lamb kebabs

The combination of lemon and oregano makes me think of craggy Greek islands – the azure-blue sea rolling into shadowed coves, the sun beating down on the dusty dry earth. Of course, if we were eating these kebabs on a Greek island, we'd be using lemons picked ripe from the tree and heady, wild oregano. Such things are not so easy to come by in the UK, but I'd like to think this recipe makes up for it by using preserved lemons, with their intense citrus flavour, while cultivated oregano still lends plenty of aroma to the dish. This is such a simple recipe to prepare, but is no less delicious for it. The grilled lemons pack quite a punch and can be eaten alongside the meat. If you'd prefer not to use lamb then chicken breasts are a good alternative. Serve with my Quinoa Tabbouleh, Chickpea Pancakes, Butter Bean Hummus with Mint Oil and Carrot and Orange Salad (see pages 66, 172, 173 and 68) for a vibrant feast.

nut free   gluten free   dairy free   egg free   soya free   yeast free

Serves 4

500g boned shoulder
  of lamb
4 preserved lemons (see the
  Glossary, page 232)
1 fat clove of garlic
Leaves from a small bunch
  of oregano
2 tbsp olive oil
1 tbsp freshly squeezed
  lemon juice
Freshly ground black pepper

Equipment
You will need 8 metal or
  bamboo skewers for
  this recipe

First, soak the bamboo skewers (if using) in water for 30 minutes – this is to prevent them burning during cooking.

Cut the lamb into 3cm chunks, then slice the lemons widthways into quarters, crush the garlic and tear up the oregano leaves. Place in a large sealable freezer bag with the olive oil and lemon juice and season with black pepper. Squeeze out any excess air, then seal the bag and massage the marinade into the lamb with your fingers. (This is by far the best way to marinate meat, allowing it to become evenly coated and sealing in the flavour.) Leave to marinate for a minimum of 1 hour or overnight. If marinating for longer than 1 hour, store in the fridge, allowing it to come to room temperature before cooking.

Preheat the grill to medium–high. Thread the meat onto the skewers, adding two slices of preserved lemon per skewer. Place under the grill and cook for 10–15 minutes, turning halfway through, or until the lamb is nicely browned on the outside but still slightly pink in the middle.

quinoa
tabbouleh

A true tabbouleh is primarily a parsley salad, spiked with lemon and olive oil and with a little bit of bulgar wheat to bulk it out – not the other way round, with the bulgar wheat taking centre stage, as so many people think of it. I realise that I'm going against the grain (pun fully intended) by using quinoa, but tabbouleh is such a delightful dish that I want everyone to be able to enjoy it. Quinoa is not dissimilar in texture to bulgar wheat, with the added benefit that it's gluten free, while the proportion of grains to fresh herbs is still relatively small, as in an authentic tabbouleh. The resulting salad is bright and luscious, and I can think of a million dishes to serve it with: Lemon and Oregano Lamb Kebabs, Poached Chicken with Walnut Sauce, Moroccan Vegetable Tagine, Lamb, Apricot and Tahini Meatballs and Lamb Burgers with Beetroot Hummus (see pages 64, 186, 142, 171 and 192), to name but a few.

---

contains nuts   nut-free option   gluten free   vegan   soya free   yeast free

Serves 4 as an accompaniment

150g quinoa
375ml water or vegetable stock (see the Glossary, page 232)
1 tbsp each of pine nuts, sunflower and pumpkin seeds (or omit the pine nuts and include extra sunflower and pumpkin seeds for a nut-free option)
A large bunch of flat-leaf parsley
A large bunch of coriander
A large bunch of mint
5 tomatoes
6 soft dried apricots
4 spring onions
Juice of 1½ lemons
4–6 tbsp extra-virgin olive oil
Sea salt flakes and freshly ground black pepper

Place the quinoa in a saucepan. Pour over the water or vegetable stock, then cover with a lid and bring to the boil before reducing the heat and leaving to simmer gently for 15 minutes or until all of the liquid has been absorbed. Remove from the heat, fluff up the grains with a fork and leave to cool completely.

Place the pine nuts (if using) and seeds in a frying pan and dry-fry over a medium–high heat, shaking the pan regularly to stop them catching, for 3–4 minutes or until lightly golden.

Finely chop all of the herbs, the tomatoes and apricots and the spring onions. Place the cooked quinoa in a large serving bowl, then mix in the herbs, spring onions, apricots and tomatoes and pour over the lemon juice and 4 tablespoons of the olive oil, adding extra oil if you think it necessary. Add the toasted pine nuts (if using) and seeds and toss together, seasoning with salt and pepper to taste, then serve.

grilled chermoula chicken with avocado quinoa salad

A mixture of spices, garlic, oil and lemon juice used in North African cooking, chermoula has a beautifully earthy colour and aroma. It would be delicious as the spice base for a tagine, sprinkled over carrots, parsnips and chicken before roasting (a favourite of mine) or as a marinade for pork tenderloin. Here I've used it as a marinade for chicken to make a gloriously flavoursome yet light supper dish. You can buy some good ready-blended chermoula spice mixtures, but the ingredients are so easy to put together yourself and well worth the effort. If using a ready-blended variety, I would mix 2 tablespoons with the garlic, brown sugar, olive oil and lemon juice.

nut free   *gluten free*   *dairy free*   *egg free*   *soya free*   *yeast free*

Serves 4

8 skinless and boneless
   chicken thighs
175g quinoa
500ml chicken or vegetable
   stock (see the Glossary,
   page 232)
2 ripe avocados
Leaves from a large bunch
   of coriander
Extra-virgin olive oil,
   for drizzling

For the chermoula
2 tsp cumin seeds
1 tsp coriander seeds
1 tsp caraway seeds
1 clove of garlic
½ tsp turmeric
¼ tsp ground cinnamon
2 tsp smoked paprika
½ tsp chilli flakes
1 tsp soft light brown sugar
Juice of 1 lemon
3 tbsp olive oil
Sea salt flakes and freshly
   ground black pepper

First, prepare the chermoula. Dry-fry the cumin, coriander and caraway seeds in a small heavy-based frying pan over a medium-high heat, shaking the pan regularly to stop them catching, for 2–3 minutes or until lightly golden and releasing their fragrant aroma. Remove from the heat and, using a pestle and mortar, grind until a fine powder. Alternatively, place in a freezer bag and crush with a rolling pin.

Crush the garlic and add to a bowl with the ground, toasted spices, ready-ground spices, chilli flakes, brown sugar, lemon juice and olive oil. Season well with salt and pepper and mix until combined.

Slice each chicken thigh widthways into 2–3 strips, depending on its size. Place in a sealable freezer bag, then add the chermoula, squeeze out any air and seal the bag. Massage the marinade into the meat through the bag before leaving to marinate for 2–3 hours or overnight. Store in the fridge if marinating for longer than 2 hours, allowing it to come up to room temperature before cooking.

When you are ready to cook the chicken, add the quinoa to a saucepan and pour over the stock, then cover with a lid and bring to the boil. Reduce the heat to low and simmer gently for about 15 minutes or until the stock has been completely absorbed. Remove from the heat, fluff up the quinoa grains with a fork and set aside.

Preheat the grill to medium–high and line the grill pan with foil.

Slice each avocado in half, discard the stone, scoop out the flesh and cut into 1cm-thick wedges. Lay in the foil-lined grill pan, along with the marinated chicken, and grill for 10–12 minutes, turning the chicken regularly, until cooked through and starting to brown at the edges. Serve immediately on a bed of quinoa with torn leaves of fresh coriander scattered over the top and a drizzle of olive oil.

al fresco

carrot &
orange salad

Bright, crunchy, zesty and packed full of sweet, citrusy flavour, this is a gloriously vibrant salad that looks and tastes like sunshine in a bowl. Enjoy it with grilled chicken or falafel for a simple lunch, or serve it as part of a larger spread. It would go particularly well with Lamb Burgers with Beetroot Hummus or with Lemon and Oregano Lamb Kebabs, Chickpea Pancakes and Butter Bean Hummus with Mint Oil (see pages 192, 64, 172 and 173). It's worth making a day ahead (or, at the very least, a few hours ahead of time) as the flavours develop wonderfully when left. Also, it's important that you finely grate the carrots by hand, as using a food processor can result in overly soggy carrots.

nut free   gluten free   vegan   soya free   yeast free

Serves 4–6 as an accompaniment

2 tbsp extra-virgin olive oil
Juice of 1 lemon
Grated zest and juice of
    1 orange
½ white onion
30g raisins
450g carrots
4 sticks of celery

Whisk together the olive oil, lemon juice, orange zest and juice until amalgamated. Halve the onion and slice into very fine half-moons, then add to the dressing with the raisins. Massage all the ingredients together with your hands and leave to soak for 10 minutes.

Peel and finely grate the carrots, then trim the celery and slice into fine rounds. Place these in a large serving bowl, pour over the dressing-soaked onion and raisins and mix everything together. Cover with a plate or cling film and leave in the fridge for at least an hour before serving.

chicken, roasted tomato & caper herb salad

Lightly poached tender chicken, oven-roasted sweet tomatoes and a piquant caper and olive oil dressing – the ingredients are simple but have such a lovely depth of flavour and range of texture that this salad has become a firm favourite of mine. It stands alone quite happily as a light lunch, but if you wish to bulk it out, serve it on a bed of Puy lentils and rocket leaves or with my Sweet Potato Bread (see page 78) on the side and a handful of black olives. Do try to use a large bunch of parsley, as it is very much an integral part of the salad rather than just a background ingredient.

nut free   gluten free   dairy free   egg free   soya free   yeast free

Serves 4

A large bunch of flat-leaf
    parsley
Juice of 1 lemon
4 skinless chicken breasts
400g tomatoes
1 tbsp olive oil
Sea salt flakes and freshly
    ground black pepper

For the dressing
¼ tsp mustard powder
2 tsp maple syrup
2 tbsp extra-virgin olive oil
2 tbsp lemon juice
2 tbsp capers, drained
    and rinsed

First, chop the leaves from the parsley stalks, retaining the stalks and setting the leaves aside for the salad. Fill a large saucepan with water up to three-quarters full, add a good pinch of salt and the lemon juice and parsley stalks, then cover with a lid and bring to the boil. Once the water is boiling, remove from the heat, add the chicken breasts, cover again with the lid and set aside for 50–55 minutes. Drain the chicken breasts in a colander and pat dry with kitchen paper.

Preheat the oven to 180°C (350°F), gas mark 4.

Slice the tomatoes into halves or quarters, depending on their size. Place in a roasting tin, drizzle with the olive oil and season well with salt and pepper. Roast for 10 minutes, then remove from the oven and set aside.

While the tomatoes are roasting, prepare the dressing. Combine the mustard powder and maple syrup in a small bowl and stir together. Pour in the olive oil, a little at a time, whisking continuously to create an emulsion, then add the lemon juice and capers and season with salt and pepper to taste.

Cut the poached chicken breasts on the diagonal into 1cm-thick slices, mix with the roasted tomatoes and reserved parsley leaves, then toss in the dressing to serve.

al fresco

roasted
vegetable socca

Socca, or farinata as it is sometimes known, is a flatbread made simply with gram flour, olive oil and water. I sometimes incorporate a little rosemary or smoked paprika, or add roasted vegetables, as in this recipe, but the bread is equally delicious without and makes a quick and easy addition to any meal. Serve with a platter of antipasti – artichokes, cured meats and garlic mushrooms spring to mind – or with soup, such as Tomato and Almond or Butternut Squash, Lentil, Honey and Thyme (see pages 185 and 178). I also like to serve it with Grilled Chermoula Chicken with Avocado Quinoa Salad, and it goes beautifully with my Lemon and Oregano Lamb Kebabs (see pages 67 and 64), a generous dollop of hummus the only addition. Cooked without the roasted vegetables, it makes a very successful pizza base: bake as below (omitting the vegetables), then layer over your choice of pizza toppings and return to the oven for a further 15–20 minutes. However you serve it, you'll find that it tastes best straight from the oven.

nut free   *gluten free*   *vegan*   *soya free*   *yeast free*

Serves 4

150g gram flour
½ tsp sea salt flakes
4 tbsp olive oil
1 orange or yellow pepper
6 sun-dried tomatoes
A few pitted black olives

Equipment
You will need a 23–25cm ovenproof frying pan for this recipe

To make the batter, place the flour in a large mixing bowl and add the salt, half the olive oil and 250ml of water. Whisk together until completely smooth, then leave to stand for 30–60 minutes.

Preheat the oven to 180°C (350°F), gas mark 4.

Cut open and deseed the pepper and slice into thin strips, then roughly chop the sun-dried tomatoes. Pour the remaining oil into the frying pan, mix in the pepper strips and roast in the oven for 15 minutes.

Remove the pan from the oven, scoop out the pepper strips with a slotted spoon and pour in the socca batter. Scatter the slightly roasted pieces of pepper over the top of the batter, along with the sun-dried tomatoes and olives, and return to the oven to bake for 30 minutes or until set and golden brown. Leave to cool for a minute or two and then use a spatula to lift it out of the pan before cutting into slices to serve.

chicken, fennel
& raisin red rice salad
salmon, new potato & pea
salad with mint pesto dressing
sweet potato bread
spiced squash,
avocado & mixed sprout salad
spiced onion muffins

light lunches

chicken with artichoke purée
salmon & avocado sushi bowls
with ginger & sesame dressing
butter bean & parsnip scones
chicory, ham, sweet
potato & sun-dried tomato salad
parsnip, chilli & lemon soup
butternut squash
& tomato muffins

chicken, fennel
& raisin red rice salad

This summertime salad is perfect for a light lunch or supper, or as part of a picnic spread. It's a great way of using up leftover roast chicken, too. I've included a sweet-sharp honey mustard dressing, which adds a lovely tang, while toasted pumpkin seeds give crunch and extra nuttiness to the rice. Carmague red rice is available in most supermarkets, but if you can't get hold of it then brown basmati or even quinoa is a good alternative.

nut free   gluten free   dairy free   egg free   soya free   yeast free

Serves 4–8

175g Camargue red rice
500ml vegetable or chicken stock (see the Glossary, page 232)
50g pumpkin seeds
¼ cucumber
1 small fennel bulb
3 sticks of celery
350g cooked chicken
A small bunch of chives
75g raisins

For the honey mustard dressing
1 tbsp English mustard (1 heaped tbsp mustard powder mixed with 1 tbsp water) or homemade mustard (see the Glossary, page 229)
1 tbsp runny honey
5 tbsp extra-virgin olive oil
1 tsp lemon juice (optional)
Sea salt flakes and freshly ground black pepper

Place the rice in a large saucepan and pour over the stock, then cover with a lid and bring to the boil. Once the stock is boiling, reduce the heat and simmer gently for 30–35 minutes or until all of the liquid has been absorbed. Set aside to cool completely.

While the rice is cooling, make the dressing. Stir together the mustard and honey until combined. Pour in the olive oil, a little at a time, stirring or whisking continuously until emulsified. Season with salt and pepper to taste and add a little lemon juice if you think it needs it.

In a heavy-based frying pan, dry-fry the pumpkin seeds over a medium–high heat, shaking the pan regularly to ensure they don't catch, for around 5 minutes or until lightly toasted.

Peel the cucumber, slice lengthways into quarters and then finely chop. Trim the ends from the fennel, cut into quarters lengthways and finely slice widthways. Trim the celery and cut into thin rounds, then chop the chicken into 1cm dice and finely chop the chives.

Once the rice has cooled, fluff up with a fork and transfer to a large serving bowl. Add the chicken to the rice with the chives, cucumber, fennel, celery, raisins and toasted pumpkin seeds and mix together. Drizzle over the honey mustard dressing and toss lightly before serving.

salmon, new potato &
pea salad with mint pesto dressing

The bright and clean flavours in this salad immediately bring to mind warm days and outdoor eating, though, of course, you can enjoy it at any time of year. The salmon imparts a smoked, salty kick to the dish and the peas a gentle sweetness, complemented by the creamy bite of the warm new potatoes, which also soak up the rich mint pesto dressing. These flavours were meant to go together and the dish needs little or no accompaniment. You can serve it immediately, the new potatoes still a little warm, or make it in advance and allow the flavours to develop and infuse – it's delicious either way. If you would like to make this dish nut free, you can use the dill and mustard dressing below instead.

contains nuts   *nut-free option*   *gluten free*   *dairy free*   *egg free*   *soya free*   *yeast free*

Serves 2–4

400g baby new potatoes
100g fresh or frozen peas
2 Little Gem lettuces
200g hot-smoked salmon

For the mint pesto dressing
50g pine nuts
Leaves from a large bunch
  of mint
Juice of ½ lemon
1 tsp agave or maple syrup
4 tbsp extra-virgin olive oil
Sea salt flakes and freshly
  ground black pepper

For the dill and mustard
dressing (nut-free option)
Grated zest and juice of
  1 lemon
A small bunch of dill
2 tsp caster sugar
¼ tsp mustard powder
2 tbsp extra-virgin olive oil
A pinch of sea salt flakes

To make the mint pesto dressing (if using), first preheat the oven to 180°C (350°F), gas mark 4.

Place the pine nuts on a baking tray and toast in the oven, turning them occasionally to ensure they don't burn, for 3–4 minutes or until lightly golden. Remove from the oven and tip into a mortar, then scatter over the mint leaves and a pinch of salt and grind to a paste with a pestle. Stir in the remaining ingredients and season with pepper and more salt to taste. Alternatively, place all the ingredients in a food processor and blitz to a paste.

For a nut-free option, make the dill and mustard dressing. Place the lemon zest and juice in a small bowl. Finely chop the dill and add it to the bowl with the remaining ingredients. Whisk together until amalgamated and set aside.

Cut the potatoes into halves or quarters, depending on their size – you want them to be in small, bite-sized chunks. Bring a saucepan of salted water to the boil and add the new potatoes. (When cooking potatoes it's useful to remember that old potatoes should be placed in cold water and brought to the boil, while new potatoes should be added to water that is already boiling.)

Gently boil the potatoes for 8–10 minutes or until tender to the point of a knife and then drain in a colander. Meanwhile, place the peas in a bowl and cover with just-boiled water, leave to sit for 5 minutes and then drain.

Trim the ends from the lettuces, removing any damaged leaves. Slice the larger leaves in half lengthways and scatter these over a serving platter or large bowl. Flake the salmon into a mixing bowl, adding the drained peas and new potatoes. Pour over the mint pesto dressing, or the dill and mustard dressing, and fold into the salmon and potatoes. Spoon the salad on top of the lettuce leaves and serve.

light lunches

sweet
potato bread

This quick, no-rise bread is so incredibly simple to make and requires only a handful of ingredients. Cooked sweet potato binds the dough, adding moisture, flavour and colour. The result is a crisp crust with a dense, soft and slightly sweet interior. It's just the thing for a relaxed lunch: serve it with soup, salad, dips or other delights. While it's at its best served straight from the oven and really doesn't last more than a day, it's ideal picnic fare. As soon as you've taken it from the oven, wrap it in foil to keep in the warmth; that way you'll have a fresh loaf to share during a lazy day in the sun. If you make the puréed sweet potato in advance, the bread will take next to no time to prepare.

nut free   gluten free   vegan   soya free   yeast free

Makes 1 loaf (to serve 8)

375g sweet potatoes (300g peeled weight)
300g gluten-free plain flour (ideally Doves Farm)
2 tsp gluten-free baking powder
½ tsp sea salt flakes
3 tbsp olive oil, plus extra for greasing

Preheat the oven to 200°C (400°F), gas mark 6, and lightly grease a baking sheet with olive oil.

Peel the sweet potatoes and cut into 2cm chunks. Bring a saucepan of salted water to the boil, add the sweet potatoes and boil gently for 10 minutes or until very tender to the point of a knife – you want them almost on the point of collapse as this will help when puréeing them. Remove from the heat and drain in a colander, then place in a food processor and blitz until completely smooth.

Place the flour, baking powder and salt in a large mixing bowl and whisk together until combined. Add the sweet potato purée, olive oil and 65ml of water and mix together until combined and forming into a ball of dough. Pull the dough together with your hands and knead very lightly for a minute or two, just to smooth it out and help bring it together.

Shape the dough into a circle about 15cm in diameter, smoothing the edges and the top with your hands. Place on the greased baking sheet and then use a sharp knife to score two crosses into the top of the loaf, each about 5mm deep, so that eight wedges are already marked before the bread goes into the oven.

Bake in the oven for 35–40 minutes or until crisp and golden. Divide into wedges and serve warm.

spiced squash, avocado & mixed sprout salad

Packed full of flavour and texture, this hearty salad is just the thing to power you through the day. The meltingly spicy squash offsets the natural crunch of the mixed sprouts (chickpea, aduki, lentil and mung bean work best), while the creamy avocado cools things down and helps balance the dish. I really adore this recipe – the perfect salad for autumn.

nut free   gluten free   vegan   soya free   yeast free

Serves 4

1 butternut squash
   (about 650g)
1 small red onion
2 tomatoes
1 tbsp olive oil
1 tsp black mustard seeds
½ tsp cumin seeds
½ tsp chilli powder
1 large ripe avocado
   (preferably Hass)
A handful of pitted black
   olives
250g mixed sprouts

For the dressing
2 tbsp extra-virgin olive oil
1 tbsp lemon juice
1 tsp soft light brown sugar
Sea salt flakes and freshly
   ground black pepper

Peel and halve the butternut squash, scoop out the seeds and pith and cut into 1.5cm chunks. Finely chop the onion and tomatoes.

Heat the olive oil in a large heavy-based saucepan or frying pan, add the mustard seeds and fry over a medium heat for 1 minute or until they begin to pop. Add the cumin seeds, chilli powder and chopped onion and fry for a further minute, stirring all the ingredients together so that they are well mixed, then cover with a lid and leave to cook for another 2 minutes.

Remove the lid and add the squash, stirring it into the onion and spices. Cover again and leave to cook over a low–medium heat for 15 minutes, stirring every now and then to stop the squash catching on the bottom of the pan.

Remove the lid and add the chopped tomatoes, stir in and cook for a further 5 minutes or until the squash is tender to the point of a knife and slightly browned on the outside. (You want to catch the squash just as it begins to turn golden but is not yet cooked to the point that it starts to fluff or collapse.) Set aside and leave to cool down completely.

Slice the avocado in two, remove the stone and scoop out the flesh from each half in one piece using a spoon. Slice the avocado into strips lengthways and roughly chop the olives. Mix together the ingredients for the dressing in a small bowl, seasoning to taste with salt and pepper.

Combine the mixed sprouts, cooked squash, avocado strips and olives in a large serving bowl, then pour over the dressing and gently toss everything together to serve.

spiced onion muffins

Mildly spicy with just a hint of background sweetness from the onions, these muffins make a delicious accompaniment to soups and salads; they're also really handy for packed lunches, picnics and snacks. They go particularly well with my Parsnip, Chilli and Lemon Soup (see page 89), and I've even served them alongside my Creamy Chicken Curry (see page 141) to good effect. Once baked, the muffins can be frozen, then simply defrosted and heated through in a hot oven before serving.

nut free   gluten free   vegan   soya free   yeast free

Makes 8 muffins

2 large onions
A generous pinch of sea salt flakes
1 tbsp good-quality curry powder of your choice
250ml rice milk
1 tbsp lemon juice
4 tbsp ground flaxseed
60ml olive oil, plus 1 tbsp for frying
300g gluten-free plain flour (ideally Doves Farm)
1 tbsp gluten-free baking powder
½ tsp bicarbonate of soda

Equipment
You will need a 12-hole muffin tin for this recipe

Halve the onions and then finely slice into half-moons. Heat 1 tablespoon of olive oil in a large, heavy-based saucepan and when the oil is hot, add the onions and sea salt (this will help stop the onions catching as they cook). Fry gently over a very low heat for about 30 minutes or until the onions are completely soft, then add the curry powder and fry for a further 3 minutes. Remove from the heat and set aside to cool.

Preheat the oven to 200°C (400°F), gas mark 6, and line the muffin tin with muffin cases or papers.

Whisk the rice milk with the lemon juice in a large mixing bowl and set aside for 5 minutes so that the lemon can sour the milk. Place the ground flaxseed in a small bowl, add 6 tablespoons of water and stir together until combined, then leave to thicken for a couple of minutes.

Add the flax mixture and the 60ml of olive oil to the soured milk and gently whisk together. Sift in the flour, baking powder and bicarbonate of soda, then add the spiced onions and fold into the mixture with a metal spoon until evenly combined.

Spoon the muffin mixture into the cases, filling them two-thirds full. Bake in the oven for 45–50 minutes or until slightly risen and golden. Leave to cool in the tin for a few minutes and either serve warm or transfer to a wire rack to cool down completely.

rolled breast of
chicken with artichoke purée

Here the piquant flavours of capers and artichokes are brought together in a simple yet elegant dish. The purée itself can be made ahead of time and could be prepared separately as a dip – it goes particularly well with my Sweet Potato Bread (see page 78), warm from the oven. I like to serve the whole dish with buttery Jersey Royal new potatoes and a green salad or creamy mashed potato, lightly braised carrots and peas – beautifully clean combinations.

nut free   *gluten free*   *dairy free*   *egg free*   *soya free*   *yeast free*

Serves 4

4 skinless chicken breasts

For the artichoke purée
1 x 280g jar of artichoke
    hearts in olive oil
1 tbsp capers, drained
    and rinsed
1 tsp English mustard
    (1 heaped tsp mustard
    powder mixed with 1 tsp
    water) or homemade
    mustard (see the Glossary,
    page 229)
Freshly ground black pepper

Preheat the oven to 200°C (400°F), gas mark 6, and cut out four 20cm squares of baking parchment.

Drain the artichoke hearts, reserving 50ml of the olive oil to use in the purée. Place the artichoke hearts, capers and mustard in a blender or food processor and blitz into a coarse purée, stopping every now and then to scrape down the sides of the blender jug or food processor bowl. Pour in the olive oil bit by bit, blitzing as you go and allowing the ingredients to amalgamate and become smooth. Season with a little pepper, then transfer to a bowl, cover with cling film or a plate and leave to chill in the fridge while you prepare the chicken.

Place two chicken breasts between two layers of cling film and use a wooden meat mallet or rolling pin to evenly beat each breast to about 5mm thick. Repeat with the remaining chicken breasts.

Spoon some of the artichoke purée onto one of the beaten chicken breasts, using the back of a spoon to spread it into a thin, even layer and leaving a 1cm gap around the edge of the meat. Take hold of one of the shorter ends of the chicken breast and carefully roll it up, encasing the purée as you go, then secure the chicken roll with two cocktail sticks, pinning the meat horizontally.

Tuck the two ends of the chicken under neatly and then place on a sheet of baking parchment and roll it up carefully so that the parchment forms a tube around the chicken. Secure by placing the chicken roll, paper seam-side down, in a roasting tin. Repeat with the remaining chicken breasts.

Roast in the oven for 25–30 minutes or until the chicken is cooked through, the juices running clear when the meat is pierced with a skewer or cocktail stick. Remove from the oven and allow the chicken to rest for 5 minutes before cutting into rounds and serving.

light lunches

nut-free option

salmon & avocado sushi bowls
with ginger & sesame dressing

This is essentially deconstructed sushi, but it tastes equally good: sticky sushi rice, smooth smoked salmon, creamy avocado and dark nori (seaweed) with its distinctive umami tang, all brought together with a light yet punchy ginger and sesame dressing. Removing the need for any fiddly rolling and wrapping makes this dish ideal for a quick and healthy lunch or supper. It's just the thing when you're out and about – to eat at your desk or on the move. You can pack it up like a bento box, each ingredient in its own section, and then pull it together when you're ready to eat. I've used smoked salmon here because I love it, but you could replace it with hot-smoked salmon fillets, smoked mackerel, prawns or any other ready-cooked fish.

contains nuts   nut-free option   gluten free   dairy free   egg free   soya free   yeast free

Serves 2

85g brown or white sushi rice
10cm piece of cucumber
1 ripe avocado (preferably Hass)
200g smoked salmon
2 sheets of nori
A handful of pea shoots or watercress sprigs (optional)
½ tbsp sesame seeds (or omit for a nut-free option)

For the ginger dressing
½ clove of garlic
2.5cm piece of root ginger
2 tbsp lemon juice
1 tsp soft light brown sugar or maple syrup
1 tbsp toasted sesame oil (or smoked olive or rapeseed oil for a nut-free option)
1 tbsp light sesame oil (or olive oil for a nut-free option)

Place the rice in a saucepan with 250ml of water, cover with a lid and bring to the boil. Once the water is boiling, reduce the heat to low and leave to simmer very gently for 25–30 minutes or until all of the liquid has been absorbed and the rice is plump and sticky. (Please note that brown sushi rice takes around 10 minutes longer to cook than white.) Set aside to cool down.

Next, make the dressing. Crush the garlic and finely grate the ginger, then place in a bowl with the lemon juice and brown sugar (or maple syrup) and stir together. Add both types of oil, whisking these in a little at a time until amalgamated.

Peel the cucumber and chop into very small dice. Slice the avocado in two and remove the stone, then use a spoon to scoop out the flesh from each half in one piece before slicing thinly lengthways. Cut the smoked salmon and nori sheets into thin strips.

Divide the cooked rice between two separate bowls and pile the cucumber, avocado, smoked salmon and pea shoots or watercress sprigs (if using) on top. Drizzle over the ginger dressing, then sprinkle over the nori strips and the sesame seeds (if using). Either serve immediately or cover in cling film and chill in the fridge until ready to eat.

butter bean
& parsnip scones

These scones are brilliant for whipping up for a simple lunch or supper. They are surprisingly quick to make and have a lovely light texture thanks to the creaminess of the butter beans, while the grated parsnip and smoked paprika add moisture and a savoury sweetness. I like to serve them warm with a hearty dish, such as my Moroccan Vegetable Tagine (see page 142) or a bowl of soup – my rich Tomato and Almond Soup would be perfect (see page 185). And I have been known to present them alongside a generous portion of my Busy Boston Baked Beans (see page 118) for a nourishing nursery–style supper. These really are best served straight from the oven, though you can freeze a batch, defrosting them as needed and heating them through in a hot oven before serving.

nut free　*gluten free*　*vegan*　*soya free*　*yeast free*

Makes 12 scones

1 large parsnip
A large bunch of chives or
　4 spring onions
175g gluten-free self-raising
　flour (ideally Doves Farm)
½ tsp smoked paprika
1 tsp gluten-free baking
　powder
1 x 400g tin of butter beans,
　drained and rinsed
½ tsp sea salt flakes
1 heaped tsp egg replacer
　(ideally Orgran) whisked
　with 2 tbsp water
4 tbsp rice milk
1 tbsp olive oil, plus extra
　for greasing

Preheat the oven to 200°C (400°F), gas mark 6, and generously grease a large baking sheet with olive oil.

Trim and peel the parsnip and finely grate in a food processor. Roughly chop the chives or spring onions and place in the food processor with the grated parsnip. Sift in the flour, paprika and baking powder, then add the remaining ingredients and blitz until the mixture forms a rough, slightly sticky dough.

Turn the dough into a mixing bowl and, using your hands, pull it together into a ball. Break off a small handful of the dough, then roll it between the palms of your hands and shape into a round patty approximately 7cm in diameter.

Place on the prepared baking sheet and press down on it lightly with the flat of your hand until about 2.5cm thick, ensuring it stays in a round shape. Repeat with the remaining dough until you have made all of the scones.

Bake in the oven for 40 minutes or until crisp and golden, turning the scones over after 20 minutes to ensure even cooking.

chicory, ham, sweet potato & sun-dried tomato salad

Chicory leaves, with their mildly bitter taste, provide the ideal basis for a slightly more grown-up salad. I like to contrast the crunch of the leaves with soft and starchy roasted sweet potato, tender smoked ham and intensely flavoured sun-dried tomatoes and capers. All these combine to make a lovely winter salad that would go beautifully with my Caramelised Onion Tart or Butter Bean and Parsnip Scones (see pages 61 and 86).

nut free *gluten free* *dairy free* *egg free* *soya free* *yeast free*

Serves 4 as an accompaniment

1 x 500g smoked ham
1 large sweet potato
1 tbsp garlic oil
2 heads of chicory
100g sun-dried tomatoes in olive oil
1 tbsp capers, drained and rinsed
Sea salt flakes and freshly ground black pepper

Place the ham in a large saucepan and cover with water (ensuring that there is at least 3cm of water above the ham). Bring to the boil, spooning off any froth that rises to the top, then reduce the heat to medium–low and leave to simmer very gently for 30 minutes or until tender and cooked through. Drain in a colander and leave to cool.

While the ham is cooling, preheat the oven to 200°C (400°F), gas mark 6.

Trim and peel the sweet potato and cut into 2cm cubes. Place in a roasting tin, pour over the garlic oil and season with salt and pepper. Roast in the oven for 30 minutes or until cooked through and golden at the edges.

Take the cooked ham and, using a fork, tear into bite-sized pieces. Trim the base from each head of chicory and peel away the leaves, laying them out on a serving platter or in a bowl.

Drain the sun-dried tomatoes, retaining the oil, and cut into thin strips. Scatter the roasted sweet potato over the chicory leaves, along with the ham, sun-dried tomatoes and capers, and drizzle over a little of the sun-dried tomato oil before serving.

parsnip, chilli & lemon soup

With their sweet flavour and creamy texture, parsnips lend themselves to being cooked with spices. Curried parsnip soup has always been my preference – until I tried this version, that is. The flavours marry together beautifully, the sweetness of the parsnip offset by the kick of the chilli, the spike of heat from the ginger, the cooling, velvety coconut milk and the light and fragrant scattering of lemon zest and coriander. Added last, the lemon zest and herbs give a deliciously fresh and aromatic note to the soup. Sustaining and invigorating at the same time, it would go particularly well with Chickpea Pancakes and Butter Bean Hummus with Mint Oil and my Watercress and Radish Salad with Avocado Dressing (see pages 172, 173 and 53).

nut free   *gluten free*   *vegan*   *soya free*   *yeast free*

Serves 4

1 white onion
1 clove of garlic
1cm piece of root ginger
500g parsnips
2 tbsp olive oil
½ tsp chilli flakes
500ml vegetable stock
    (see the Glossary,
    page 232)
200ml coconut milk
Grated zest and juice of
    1 lemon
A small bunch of coriander
Sea salt flakes and freshly
    ground black pepper

Finely chop the onion and garlic and peel the ginger, then trim and peel the parsnips and cut into 1cm dice. Heat the olive oil in a large saucepan, add the onion and garlic and fry over a low–medium heat for about 8 minutes or until just soft but not browned. Stir in the chilli flakes and a good pinch of salt, finely grate in the ginger and continue to fry for a further minute.

Add the parsnips to the onion mixture, then cover with a lid and fry gently for 10 minutes or until the parsnips start to soften, stirring every now and then to stop them catching on the bottom of the pan. Pour over the vegetable stock and bring to the boil, then reduce the heat to low and leave to simmer gently for a further 15 minutes.

Pour the coconut milk and lemon juice into the soup, scatter over the lemon zest and then, using a hand-held blender or food processor, blitz until completely smooth and velvety. If at this point you think the soup seems a little too thick, simply add dashes of boiling water until it has reached the desired consistency. Season with salt and pepper to taste, then finely chop the coriander and sprinkle a little over each bowl before serving.

butternut squash
& tomato muffins

These light and fluffy muffins are a real savoury treat. They're versatile, too – ideal for breakfast or supper as well as lunch. The butternut squash is roasted until fragrant and tender, combined with the tomatoes and then folded into the muffin batter and baked until risen and golden. The result is a delicious medley of textures, perfect for serving with baked beans and sliced tomatoes for breakfast, or simply with a knob of dairy-free margarine. These muffins make a delicious accompaniment to soups and certain stews, or even a slow-cooked Chilli con Carne (see page 154). If you don't want to include the tomatoes, you can replace them with smoked lardons, fried until crispy, and you can add spices to the batter if you like: a pinch of chilli flakes or smoked paprika would work well.

nut free   gluten free   vegan   soya free   yeast free

Makes 8 muffins

400g butternut squash
   (350g peeled weight)
250ml rice milk
1 tbsp lemon juice
4 tbsp ground flaxseed
60ml olive oil, plus 1 tbsp
   for roasting
100g sun-dried tomatoes
300g gluten-free plain flour
   (ideally Doves Farm)
1 tbsp gluten-free baking
   powder
½ tsp bicarbonate of soda
Sea salt flakes and freshly
   ground black pepper

Equipment
You will need a 12-hole muffin
   tin for this recipe

Preheat the oven to 200°C (400°F), gas mark 6, and fill the muffin tin with muffin cases or papers.

Peel the butternut squash and scoop out any seeds or pith. Cut into 1cm cubes and place in a roasting tin with 1 tablespoon of olive oil and stir together until evenly coated. Season well with salt and pepper and roast in the oven for 40 minutes or until tender and golden.

Meanwhile, whisk the rice milk with the lemon juice in a large mixing bowl and set aside for 5 minutes so that the lemon can sour the milk. Place the ground flaxseed in a small bowl, add 6 tablespoons of water and stir together until combined. Roughly chop the sun-dried tomatoes and set aside.

Add the flax mixture and the 60ml of olive oil to the soured milk and gently whisk together. Sift in the flour, baking powder and bicarbonate of soda, then add the roasted squash and sun-dried tomatoes and season well with salt and pepper. Fold all the ingredients together using a metal spoon until evenly combined.

Fill the muffin cases two-thirds full with the mixture. Bake in the oven for 45–50 minutes or until slightly risen and golden. Leave to cool in the tin for a few minutes and either serve warm or transfer to a wire rack to cool down completely.

parsnip & apple
cake with orange icing
honey & blueberry
drizzle cake
lemon curd
chocolate
malted muffins
lemon &
coconut tartlets
rhubarb &
apple traybake
carrot & ginger
squares with lemon icing
st clement's cake
gingerbread loaf
spiced apple cake
vanilla bundt cake
chocolate
celebration cake
lemon butterfly cakes

lazy
Afternoons

parsnip & apple
cake with orange icing

I've often extolled the virtues of incorporating vegetables in baking, not least because using them can leave you feeling distinctly virtuous. Including them in the mix has other benefits, too, adding flavour, moisture and texture to your baking. This recipe combines parsnips with a little apple, soft brown sugar and flaxseed to create a rich, moist cake, perfect for topping with a layer of zesty orange icing. Due, no doubt, to the orange and parsnips (both traditionally winter fare), this cake has a very Christmassy feel and I like to bring it out during the festive season.

nut free   gluten free   vegan   soya free   yeast free

Serves 8–12

150g dairy-free margarine,
    plus extra for greasing
100ml agave or golden
    syrup
200g soft light brown sugar
250g parsnips
1 eating apple
100g apple purée (see the
    Glossary, page 225)
250g gluten-free self-raising
    flour (ideally Doves Farm)
3 tsp gluten-free baking
    powder
½ tsp mixed spice
25g ground flaxseed

For the icing
150g icing sugar
2–3 tbsp orange juice
Grated zest of 1 orange

Equipment
You will need a deep,
    20cm round cake tin with
    a removable base for this
    recipe

Preheat the oven to 180°C (350°F), gas mark 4, and lightly grease and line the cake tin.

Place the margarine, agave or golden syrup and brown sugar in a saucepan and heat gently over a low heat, stirring every now and then, until combined and the sugar has completely dissolved. Meanwhile, trim the ends from the parsnips and peel. Core the apple and peel. Coarsely grate both the apple and the parsnips – I would highly recommend you do this by hand, as using a food processor can affect the water content of the vegetables and therefore the cake. Set aside.

Transfer the syrup mixture to a large mixing bowl and leave to cool for 5 minutes before stirring in the apple purée. Next, sift in the flour, baking powder and mixed spice and gently fold into the syrup mixture. Add the grated parsnip, apple and ground flaxseed and fold through until combined. Pour the mixture into the cake tin and bake in the oven for 1 hour–1 hour 10 minutes or until risen and golden and firm to the touch when pressed lightly with a fingertip.

Leave the cake to cool in the tin for 5 minutes and then transfer to a wire rack to cool completely. Once cooled, make up the icing by sifting the icing sugar into a bowl and adding the orange juice, bit by bit, until the desired consistency. Spread over the top of the cake, letting it run down the sides, and scatter over the orange zest.

honey &
blueberry drizzle cake

Sweet, fragrant and delicious, this cake conjures up the scents and golden haze of summer – nectar-laden blossom, ripe berries and glinting rays of sunshine. It is just the thing to serve on a balmy afternoon. Included in both the drizzle and the sponge, honey imbues the whole cake with its distinctive aroma. A hint of lemon zest and juice balances the syrupiness, while plump blueberries add bursts of vibrant colour and delicate flavour. Once made, the cake will keep for up to three days if stored in an airtight container.

nut free   *gluten free*   *dairy free*   *egg free*   *soya free*   *yeast free*

Serves 8

200g runny honey
65ml sunflower oil, plus extra for greasing
4 round tbsp apple purée (see the Glossary, page 225)
Grated zest of 1 lemon
250g gluten-free self-raising flour (ideally Doves Farm)
1 tsp gluten-free baking powder
150g fresh blueberries

For the drizzle
1 tbsp lemon juice
2 tbsp runny honey

Equipment
You will need a 900g (11cm x 22cm) loaf tin for this recipe

Preheat the oven to 180°C (350°F), gas mark 4, then lightly grease the loaf tin with sunflower oil and line with baking parchment.

Beat together the honey and sunflower oil until amalgamated, then stir in the apple purée and lemon zest. Sift in the flour and baking powder and fold in until smooth and glossy, then gently fold in the blueberries.

Tip the mixture into the prepared loaf tin, levelling the top with a spoon, and bake for 35–45 minutes or until firm to the touch and golden. Remove from the oven and place the cake, still in its tin, on a wire rack to cool.

As the cake is cooling, mix all of the ingredients for the drizzle together with 1 tablespoon of hot water until combined. While the cake is still warm but no longer hot, use a cocktail stick or fork to prick holes in the top. Spoon over the drizzle and leave the cake in the tin to cool down completely before removing to serve.

lemon
curd

Intensely zesty in flavour and smoothly unctuous in texture, this lemon curd is incredibly simple to make and very versatile. It works wonderfully in both my Lemon and Coconut Tartlets and Lemon Butterfly Cakes (see pages 100 and 113), for instance. You can also use it as an accompaniment to fresh berries for a summery pudding or fold it into whipped coconut cream or coconut yoghurt for a divinely citrusy lemon fool.

nut free   gluten free   vegan   soya free   yeast free

Makes 150g

1½ tsp cornflour
Grated zest and juice of
   1 lemon
85g golden caster sugar
70g dairy-free margarine

Place the cornflour in a small bowl and mix with a little of the lemon juice until smooth. Put the remaining ingredients into a small saucepan and cook over a low heat until the sugar has dissolved, whisking every now and then to help it along. Add the cornflour mixture to the pan and whisk it in.

Heat the mixture until it comes to a gentle boil, then whisk continuously for 1–2 minutes or until the curd has thickened enough to coat the back of a spoon. Pour into a bowl and set aside to cool down. Once the curd has cooled, cover with cling film and place in the fridge – stored like this, it will keep for up to a week.

chocolate
malted muffins

These little indulgent numbers are everything a chocolate muffin should be: fat and round on the outside and fluffily light in the middle, their cocoa-bean colour hinting at the rich flavour contained in each bite. The ground flaxseed imparts a mellow maltiness while also binding the mixture together in lieu of eggs. And the light and dark brown sugar enhance the overall flavour without being overly sweet. I just love these muffins and they are an absolute breeze to prepare, making them ideal for a quick baked treat. They freeze well, too: simply allow to defrost and then warm through in the oven before serving.

nut free   gluten free   vegan   soya free   yeast free

Makes 12 muffins

4 tbsp ground flaxseed
¼ tsp gluten-free baking powder
200g gluten-free self-raising flour (ideally Doves Farm)
4 tbsp cocoa powder
100g soft light brown sugar
100g soft dark brown sugar
120g dairy-free margarine
125ml rice milk

Equipment
You will need a 12-hole muffin tin for this recipe

Preheat the oven to 150°C (300°F), gas mark 2, and line the muffin tin with muffin cases or papers.

Begin by making up the flaxseed mixture. Place the ground flaxseed and baking powder in a small bowl, add 6 tablespoons of water and stir together until you have a liquid paste, then leave for a minute or two. In that time the flaxseed will suck up most of the moisture and become very thick and dense – it is now ready to use.

Sift the flour and cocoa powder into a large mixing bowl, add the light and dark brown sugar and stir until combined. Cut the margarine into cubes and then add to the flour mixture. Rub everything together with your fingertips until breadcrumb-like in consistency.

Add the flaxseed mixture and rice milk to the batter and beat together until thick and combined. Spoon the mixture into the muffin cases, filling each two-thirds full and smoothing over the tops.

Bake for 30 minutes until well risen and fragrant, then remove from the oven, transfer to a wire rack and allow to cool before serving – if you can wait that long!

lazy afternoons

lemon &
coconut tartlets

These delightful little tarts are just the thing to serve for afternoon tea, a children's party or a picnic. Consisting of a light shortcrust pastry filled with intensely flavoured lemon curd and topped with a crisp coconut crumb, they are a divine medley of tangy sweetness and melting crunch that will appeal to both adults and children alike. Made with gluten- and dairy-free pastry, they are also the perfect vehicle for my homemade intolerance-friendly Lemon Curd (see page 97). Stored in an airtight container, they will keep for up to three days.

nut free   gluten free   vegan   soya free   yeast free

Makes 12 tartlets

For the shortcrust pastry
115g gluten-free plain flour
    (ideally Doves Farm)
¼ tsp xanthan gum
30g vegetable shortening
30g dairy-free margarine
1 tbsp golden caster sugar

For the filling
50g golden caster sugar
50g dairy-free margarine
1 heaped tsp egg replacer
    (ideally Orgran) whisked
    with 2 tbsp water
50g desiccated coconut
1 portion of Lemon Curd
    (see page 97)

Equipment
You will need a 12-hole tart
    tin and an 8cm round
    pastry cutter for this
    recipe

Preheat the oven to 200°C (400°F), gas mark 6.

Sift the flour and xanthan gum into the bowl of a food processor. Cut the vegetable shortening into cubes and add to the flour with the margarine and sugar. Pulse until the mixture is of a breadcrumb-like consistency. Alternatively, use a large mixing bowl and rub the ingredients together with your fingertips.

Add 1 tablespoon of cold water, pulsing as you go (or stirring with a flat-bladed knife if making the pastry by hand), until the mixture begins to pull together to form a dough. You can then add an extra tablespoon of water if you think it needs it. Turn the pastry into a large mixing bowl (or keep in the same bowl, if making by hand) and, using your fingertips, pull together into a ball. Knead lightly for about 2 minutes or until smooth and elastic to your touch.

Shape the pastry into a ball and place between two sheets of cling film. Gently roll the pastry out to 3–5mm thick, then remove the top layer of cling film and stamp out 12 circles using the cutter, balling and rerolling the pastry as necessary. Carefully line the tart tin with the pastry cases and then set aside while you prepare the filling.

Place the sugar and margarine in a mixing bowl and, using a wooden spoon, cream together until light and fluffy. Stir in the egg replacer mixture and desiccated coconut until combined.

Spoon a heaped teaspoon of the lemon curd into the base of each tartlet and smooth flat with the back of the spoon. Top each tart with a teaspoon of the coconut mixture and press down gently with the spoon to ensure the top is evenly covered.

Bake in the oven for 15–18 minutes or until the pastry is crisp and the tops of the tarts are lightly golden. Remove from the tin and transfer to a wire rack, leaving to cool before serving.

rhubarb &
apple traybake

I rarely think of putting apple and rhubarb together and yet they make perfect bedfellows, the fruity sweetness of the apple purée in the sponge marrying so well with the hint of tartness from the rhubarb. Dare I say it, this is one of my favourite sweet recipes. It's so versatile, too: you can serve it warm with homemade custard (see page 213) for a comforting pudding, or leave it to cool and present it alongside a cup of tea. However you serve it, it should fit the bill with its glorious caramel-flavoured crust and soft, apple-spiked interior, offset by tangy bursts of flavour from the nuggets of roasted rhubarb. Irresistible, indeed!

nut free   *gluten free*   *vegan*   *soya free*   *yeast free*

Serves 12

400g rhubarb
100g apple purée (see the Glossary, page 225)
200g golden caster sugar, plus 2 tbsp for roasting the rhubarb
125ml sunflower oil, plus extra for greasing
1 tsp vanilla extract
225g gluten-free self-raising flour (ideally Doves Farm)
1 tsp gluten-free baking powder

Equipment
You will need an 18cm square baking tin for this recipe

Preheat the oven to 180°C (350°F), gas mark 4, then lightly grease the baking tin with sunflower oil and line with baking parchment.

Trim the ends from the rhubarb and cut into 2.5cm pieces. Place in a roasting tin, scatter over 2 tablespoons of caster sugar and roast for 15 minutes or until the rhubarb pieces are tender but still holding their shape.

Place the apple purée in a large mixing bowl with the 200g of caster sugar, the sunflower oil and vanilla extract and beat together until combined. Sift in the flour and baking powder and fold into the mixture until you have a smooth and thick batter.

Tip the batter into the prepared baking tin and smooth into the corners, levelling the top with the back of a spoon. Scatter the rhubarb evenly over the surface of the mixture and, using your fingertips, gently press the pieces down into the batter a little.

Bake for 45 minutes or until fragrant, golden and firm to the touch. Remove from the oven and either serve warm with custard (see page 213) or leave to cool completely in the tin before cutting into squares.

lazy afternoons

carrot & ginger
squares with lemon icing

Tea and cake are a bit of a treat, there's no denying it, and these little iced squares are just the thing for such an occasion. The carrot gives this gingerbread a lovely gooey texture, complemented by the zesty lemon icing with its vibrant tang. These cakes are the perfect foil to a pot of tea and a good chat with friends, although I have been known to serve them as a pudding during the winter months, minus the icing but topped with a generous pouring of custard (see page 213) instead.

nut free   gluten free   vegan   soya free   yeast free

Serves 12

150g carrots (100g trimmed and peeled weight)
200g gluten-free self-raising flour (ideally Doves Farm)
1 tsp bicarbonate of soda
1 tsp ground ginger
200g soft light brown sugar
55g dairy-free margarine, plus extra for greasing
2 tbsp golden syrup
1 heaped tsp egg replacer (ideally Orgran) whisked with 2 tbsp water

For the icing
100g icing sugar
1–2 tbsp lemon juice

Equipment
You will need an 18cm square tin for this recipe

Preheat the oven to 180°C (350°F), gas mark 4, then grease the baking tin with margarine and line with baking parchment.

Trim and peel the carrots and finely grate them. (I don't recommend you use a food processor to grate them as they retain so much water and can make the cake soggy.) Sift the flour, bicarbonate of soda and ground ginger into a large mixing bowl, add the brown sugar and grated carrots and stir together until evenly combined.

Cut the margarine into small chunks and add to the bowl. Using your hands, rub the margarine into the flour mixture until the consistency of fine breadcrumbs. Add the golden syrup and egg replacer mixture and pour over 240ml of hot water. Stir everything together with a wooden spoon until smooth and combined and then pour the batter into the lined baking tin.

Bake in the oven for 35 minutes or until golden and fragrant and the top is springy to a light touch. Leave the cake to cool in the tin while you make the icing.

Sift the icing sugar into a mixing bowl, add the lemon juice and stir together until smooth. When the cake has cooled completely, remove from the tin and spread the icing over the top. Leave to set for 20 minutes or so before cutting into squares to serve.

st clement's cake

Oranges and lemons – what better combination for this light and zesty recipe? It has all the intensity of a lemon drizzle cake but with added tang from the marmalade and a robust, mellow sweetness from the soft brown sugar. It's also a rather nifty way of finishing off any marmalade left lurking in a jar in your cupboard, although you would be hard pushed to tell it has been included – the flavours meld together in a very natural way. I really do count this as one of my all-time favourite cakes; it's just right for an afternoon get-together, with a pot of fragrant tea and a group of friends and family to share it with.

nut free   gluten free   vegan   soya free   yeast free

Serves 8

175g light soft brown sugar
150g dairy-free margarine,
    plus extra for greasing
3 heaped tsp egg replacer
    (ideally Orgran) whisked
    with 6 tbsp water
75g marmalade
Grated zest and juice of
    1 lemon
175g gluten-free self-raising
    flour (ideally Doves Farm)

For the icing
100g golden icing sugar
2 tbsp lemon juice

Equipment
You will need a 900g
    (11cm x 22cm) loaf tin
    for this recipe

Preheat the oven to 180°C (350°F), gas mark 4, then lightly grease the loaf tin with margarine and line with baking parchment.

Using a wooden spoon, cream together the sugar and margarine until combined and light and fluffy in texture. Stir in the egg replacer mixture, bit by bit. (Don't be alarmed if the batter looks as if it's beginning to split – the flour will put it back together.) Stir in the marmalade and lemon zest until evenly mixed.

Sift in the flour, add the lemon juice and, using a metal spoon, fold these into the mixture until smooth and combined. Tip the cake batter into the prepared loaf tin and level the top of the cake with the back of the spoon.

Bake for 35–40 minutes until slightly risen and golden. Remove from the oven and leave for a few minutes in the tin, then transfer to a wire rack and allow to cool while you make the icing.

Once the cake has cooled, sift the icing sugar into a mixing bowl, add the lemon juice and mix until smooth and glossy. (Please note that this is quite a runny icing; if you prefer yours thicker, just add a little extra icing sugar.) Drizzle the icing over the top and leave to set before cutting into slices to serve.

gingerbread loaf

This particular gingerbread has to be one of the easiest things in the world to prepare. In a matter of minutes you can have it in the oven, a bit of measuring and stirring your only chore, which makes it ideal for rustling up at short notice. It's what you might call 'rustic' in appearance – I've yet to bake it without the top cracking a little – but this does nothing to diminish the gorgeous ginger flavour, with just a hint of citrus from the lemon juice and caramel sweetness from the soft brown sugar. And while it might look dense, the cake is actually very light in texture. All in all, it's perfect for afternoon tea or to pack into a lunchbox for a treat at school or work. You could ice it if you wish, with lemon icing (see page 104), for instance; it would make it look a little prettier, but I really wouldn't bother unless I was serving it to guests. I rather like its homely appearance; it reminds you that it's homemade and full of good-quality, simple ingredients – just as it should be.

nut free   gluten free   vegan   soya free   yeast free

Serves 8

275g gluten-free self-raising flour (ideally Doves Farm)
1 tbsp ground ginger
1 tsp gluten-free baking powder
200g soft light brown sugar
100ml sunflower oil, plus extra for greasing
2 tbsp lemon juice

Equipment
You will need a 900g (11cm x 22cm) loaf tin for this recipe

Preheat the oven to 200°C (400°F), gas mark 6, then lightly grease the loaf tin with sunflower oil and line with baking parchment.

Sift the flour, ginger and baking powder into a large mixing bowl, add the sugar and stir together until combined. Pour in the sunflower oil, lemon juice and 170ml of water and stir together until you have a smooth batter.

Tip the mixture into the prepared loaf tin, levelling the top with the back of a spoon, and bake for 30–35 minutes or until golden and a cocktail stick or skewer inserted into the middle of the loaf comes out clean. Leave to cool in the tin for 10 minutes and then transfer to a wire rack to cool down fully before cutting up to serve.

spiced apple cake

Rich, fruity and moist with an indulgently fudgy texture, this is a serious cake, just right for a celebration or a very special afternoon tea. I use Bramley cooking apples to give a juicy base to the cake, while apple purée adds further fruity flavour and works as a brilliant substitute for eggs in pulling the sponge together. Enjoy the cake fresh or bake a few days in advance to eat later – it does actually improve a little with age. Either way, serve with a little icing sugar dusted on top.

nut free   gluten free   vegan   soya free   yeast free

Serves 8–12

2 Bramley apples
125g dairy-free margarine, plus extra for greasing
175g soft dark brown sugar
100g apple purée (see the Glossary, page 225)
225g gluten-free plain flour (ideally Doves Farm)
3 tsp gluten-free baking powder
1 heaped tsp ground cinnamon
1 heaped tsp mixed spice
Icing sugar, for dusting

Equipment
You will need a deep, 20cm round cake tin with a removable base for this recipe

Preheat the oven to 170°C (325°F), gas mark 3, then lightly grease the cake tin with margarine and line the base with baking parchment.

Peel and core the apples and chop into 5mm cubes. Place the margarine and brown sugar in a large mixing bowl and, using a wooden spoon, cream together until incorporated and light and fluffy in texture, then stir in the apple purée.

Next, sift in the flour, baking powder, cinnamon and mixed spice. Fold into the fat and sugar mixture until smooth and glossy and then fold in the apple pieces, making sure they are evenly distributed.

Tip the mixture into the prepared cake tin, levelling the top with the back of a spoon, and bake in the oven for 1 hour or until golden brown, fragrant and pulling away from the sides of the tin slightly.

Allow to cool in the tin for 20 minutes before transferring to a wire rack and leaving to cool completely, then dust with icing sugar to serve. If kept in an airtight container, it will last for up to five days.

vanilla bundt cake

This is a big and fluffy celebration cake, perfect for serving to lots of guests as part of a special afternoon spread. In fact, it's just the sort of recipe that would suit a children's party: you could easily substitute the bundt tin for a themed cake tin of your choice, as there would be plenty of batter to fill it. The apple purée keeps the cake moist and adds to the sweetness, while the vanilla gives a mellow background note. You could, if you so wished, swap the vanilla in the cake and icing for the zest and juice of two lemons (using one in the cake and one in the icing) to make a citrus version. While this cake is best served on the day it is made, it will keep for up two days in an airtight container.

nut free   gluten free   vegan   soya free   yeast free

Serves 12

400ml rice milk
200g apple purée (see Glossary, page 225)
185ml sunflower oil, plus extra for greasing
1 tbsp lemon juice
2 tsp vanilla extract
500g gluten-free plain flour (ideally Doves Farm)
2 tsp gluten-free baking powder
1 tsp bicarbonate of soda
300g golden caster sugar

For the icing
100g icing sugar
1 tsp vanilla extract
4–5 tsp rice milk

Equipment
You will need a 23cm bundt tin for this recipe

Preheat the oven to 180°C (350°F), gas mark 4, and lightly grease the bundt tin with sunflower oil.

Add the rice milk to a large mixing bowl with the apple purée, sunflower oil, lemon juice and vanilla extract and whisk together. Sift in the flour, baking powder and bicarbonate of soda, pour over the caster sugar and gently whisk it all together until smooth and glossy.

Pour the cake batter into the tin and bake in the oven for 50–55 minutes or until risen and golden and a cocktail stick or skewer inserted into the middle of the cake comes out clean. Remove from the oven and leave to cool in the tin for 10 minutes before turning out onto a wire rack to cool down fully.

Once the cake has cooled, sift the icing sugar into a mixing bowl, add the vanilla extract and rice milk and stir together until smooth, then drizzle the icing over the cake.

lazy afternoons

chocolate celebration cake

This is a true celebration cake, ideal for birthdays or parties or whenever nothing but chocolate cake will do. A layer of raspberry jam is sandwiched between two chocolate sponges, rich and gooey chocolate ganache is used to slather the top of the cake, while fresh raspberries provide decoration and just a hint of tartness. If you wanted, you could replace the jam filling with my vanilla buttercream (see page 48), and for a seriously indulgent cake you could double the quantities of ganache and spread it over the whole cake!

nut free   *gluten free*   *vegan*   *soya free*   *yeast free*

Serves 12

500ml rice milk
1 tbsp lemon juice
350g golden caster sugar
160ml sunflower oil, plus
    extra for greasing
2 tsp vanilla extract
260g gluten-free plain flour
    (ideally Doves Farm)
140g cocoa powder
1½ tsp bicarbonate of soda
1 tsp gluten-free baking
    powder
A pinch of sea salt flakes
4–5 tbsp raspberry jam
150g fresh raspberries,
    to decorate

For the ganache
80ml rice milk
225g dairy- and soya-free
    dark chocolate
3 tbsp maple syrup

Equipment
You will need two 20cm
    round cake tins with
    removable bases for
    this recipe

Preheat the oven to 180°C (350°F), gas mark 4, and lightly grease the cake tins with sunflower oil and line the bases with baking parchment.

In a large mixing bowl, whisk together the rice milk and lemon juice and then set aside for 5 minutes so that the lemon can sour the milk. (If the milk looks as if it is separating, don't worry – adding the other ingredients will bring it back together.) Pour the caster sugar, sunflower oil and vanilla extract in with the soured milk and gently whisk together.

In a separate large mixing bowl, sift together the flour, cocoa powder, bicarbonate of soda and baking powder and add the salt. Pour the liquid ingredients into the flour mixture a bit at a time, mixing everything together as you go, until you have a smooth batter.

Divide the cake batter evenly between the two prepared tins and then bake in the oven for 30–35 minutes or until fragrant and firm to the touch and a cocktail stick or skewer inserted into the centre of each cake comes out clean. Remove from the oven, leave to cool in the tins for a few minutes and transfer to a wire rack to finish cooling down.

continues...

While the cakes are cooling, make the ganache. Place the rice milk in a small saucepan and bring just to the boil. Immediately lower the heat to a simmer, then break the chocolate into pieces and add to the rice milk with the maple syrup and stir together. Take the mixture off the heat and gently whisk together until completely melted and smoothly mixed. Set aside to cool for 30 minutes before using.

Place the base layer of the cake on a platter or stand and spread over the raspberry jam. Sandwich with the second sponge and then pour the chocolate ganache over the top of the cake, letting it run a little down the sides if you like. Decorate with the fresh raspberries and then chill in the fridge to allow the ganache topping to set before serving.

lemon
butterfly cakes

Popular with children and adults alike, these sweet and citrusy butterfly cakes are perfect for afternoon tea or a birthday party. They are also exceptionally easy to make, the lemon curd giving real intensity of flavour to what is otherwise a very simple little cake. If you don't want to make them into butterfly cakes, however, you can simply leave them whole and top with a cream frosting, such as the one used for my Strawberry and Cream Cupcakes (see page 48).

nut free   *gluten free*   *vegan*   *soya free*   *yeast free*

Makes 12 cakes

100g dairy-free margarine
150g golden caster sugar
200g gluten-free self-raising flour (ideally Doves Farm)
2 tsp gluten-free baking powder
Grated zest of 1 lemon
200ml rice or other dairy-free milk of your choice
1 portion of Lemon Curd (see page 97)
Icing sugar, for dusting

Equipment
You will need a 12-hole muffin or cupcake tin for this recipe

Preheat the oven to 180°C (350°F), gas mark 4, and line the muffin or cupcake tin with paper cases.

Place the margarine and sugar in a large mixing bowl and cream together using a wooden spoon. Sift in the flour and baking powder, add the lemon zest and pour over the rice or other milk, then stir together into a smooth and creamy batter.

Divide the cake mixture evenly between the cupcake cases, levelling the tops with the back of a spoon. Bake for about 15 minutes or until golden and fragrant, then remove from the oven and transfer to a wire rack to cool down fully.

Once the cakes are completely cool, use a sharp knife to cut a circle out from the top of each one, cutting about 5mm in from the outer edge of the cake. Cut the sponge circle in half to make two little 'butterfly wings'. Spoon 1–2 teaspoons of lemon curd into the cut-out hole and then place the 'wings' on top. Sift over a little icing sugar and serve.

chicken nuggets
with barbecue sauce
busy boston
baked beans
piquant potato wedges
roasted tomato
& basil sauce
macaroni cheese
spaghetti & meatballs
pizza breads
creamy garlic, herb &
crispy bacon stuffed potatoes
shepherd's pie
fish pie
bang bang chicken

Family favourites

chicken nuggets
with barbecue sauce

Tender chicken fillets in a crisp golden coating, these nuggets are distinctly moreish. Lightly covered in gluten-free flour and a little olive oil before being baked in the oven, they're healthier than your average nugget, too. They would be ideal as a light supper with a bowl of salad on the side – Carrot and Orange, perhaps (see page 68) – or a portion of baked beans. Served either way, they'll soon be polished off – by adults and children alike.

nut free   *gluten free*   *dairy free*   *egg free*   *soya free*   *yeast free*

Serves 4 as a main dish or 8 as nibbles

20g gluten-free plain flour (ideally Doves Farm)
20g gram flour
⅛ tsp mustard powder
¼ tsp smoked paprika
½ tsp sea salt flakes
¼ tsp freshly ground black pepper
4 skinless chicken breasts
1 heaped tsp egg replacer (ideally Orgran) whisked with 2 tbsp water
3 tbsp olive oil

For the barbecue sauce
1 onion
1 clove of garlic
1cm piece of root ginger
1 tbsp olive oil
100g tomato purée
60ml apple juice
1 tbsp tamarind paste
¼ tsp mustard powder
1 tbsp lemon juice
1 tbsp maple syrup

First, make the barbecue sauce. Finely chop the onion, crush the garlic and finely grate the ginger. Heat the olive oil in a small saucepan, add the onion and garlic and sauté very gently over a low heat for about 15 minutes or until completely soft but not browned.

Tip in the grated ginger and sauté for a further 2 minutes. Add the tomato purée and then whisk in the apple juice until blended. Add all of the remaining ingredients and bring to the boil, then reduce the heat and simmer gently for 15 minutes until the sauce has thickened and reduced slightly. Remove from the heat and set aside to cool.

Meanwhile, preheat the oven to 220°C (425°F), gas mark 7, and line a baking sheet with baking parchment.

Sift the plain flour into a large mixing bowl with the gram flour, mustard powder and paprika and add the salt and black pepper. Slice the chicken breasts into 4cm chunks and place in the bowl ready to mix.

Whisk together the egg replacer mixture and the olive oil in a separate bowl and set aside.

Using your hands, mix the chicken pieces into the flour until well and evenly coated. Pour over the oil and egg replacer mixture (this may seem an odd instruction, but it is this that helps the nuggets get truly golden and crunchy on the outside) and mix in the chicken pieces with your hands to ensure they are coated all over in the mixture. (The nuggets may feel quite wet, but this is absolutely fine.)

Tip the chicken nuggets onto the lined baking sheet, making sure they're spaced out in one even layer. Bake in the oven for 15–20 minutes or until crisp and golden and the chicken is cooked through. Leave to rest for 1 minute and then serve with the sauce.

busy boston baked beans

Customarily, Boston baked beans consist of a combination of dried beans, spices, molasses and pork belly cooked for hours to produce the characteristic intensely smoky flavour. In this version of the recipe, I've replaced the pork belly with two thick slabs of smoked bacon, which adds a gorgeous flavour and, using tinned instead of dried beans, takes far less time to cook – it's ready to eat within the hour, in fact. I love to serve the beans with a big wedge of Cornbread (see page 156), but they would go just as well with slices of toasted gluten-free bread, such as my Chickpea Bread (see page 28), or a big, steaming baked potato. Equally, you could serve them as part of a cooked breakfast with my Potato Farls (see page 26) – you'd be very popular on a Sunday morning, I promise! And if you wanted to, you could make a vegetarian version by simply leaving out the smoked bacon and adding ½ teaspoon of smoked paprika instead – the dish would still taste wonderfully comforting.

nut free   *gluten free*   *dairy free*   *egg free*   *soya free*   *yeast free*

Serves 4 as an accompaniment

- 2 smoked bacon steaks or 6 rashers of smoked back bacon
- 1 white onion
- 1 clove of garlic
- 1 tbsp olive oil
- 2 x 200g tin of mixed beans, drained and rinsed
- 200ml passata (or the drained juice from a tin of chopped tomatoes, topped up with water if necessary and reserving the tomatoes for another dish)
- 1 heaped tsp mustard powder
- 1 tbsp soft dark brown sugar
- 1 tbsp black treacle
- 2 tbsp tomato purée
- 1 small bay leaf
- Sea salt flakes and freshly ground black pepper

Preheat the oven to 140°C (275°F), gas mark 1.

Slice the bacon steaks into cubes or the rashers of bacon into thin slices, depending on which you are using. Finely chop the onion and garlic and set aside.

Pour the olive oil into a casserole dish and place over a medium heat. Once the oil is hot, add the bacon and fry until golden and nearly crisp. Scoop out the bacon with a slotted spoon, setting this to one side, then reduce the heat and add the onion and garlic to the dish. Season well with salt and pepper and fry gently for 15 minutes or until soft but not browned, then add the beans, stirring them in to warm through.

Pour over the passata and add the mustard powder, sugar, black treacle, tomato purée and bay leaf. Gently stir the sauce into the beans until all the ingredients are combined. Stir in the cooked bacon, then cover the dish with its lid and cook in the oven for 1 hour, checking intermittently that the beans haven't become dry. If you think they have, then add a dash of water and continue to cook.

piquant
potato wedges

There is nothing more comforting or indulgent than a hot bowl of chips, yet so often they have been coated in a wheat-based powder and hence are completely off limits to anyone who is gluten intolerant. Not so with these wedges, which are so simple to make and taste really good, especially with the hint of spice from the paprika. Truly, there is nothing better to serve with a chargrilled steak than these, though you could eat them on their own, sprinkled with a little sea salt and with your choice of dip alongside. Don't be panicked by their appearance in the first stages of cooking – they will crisp up to become golden and crunchy, so do persevere. I recommend using Maris Piper, Lady Balfour or King Edward potatoes, as they have the ideal floury texture for chips, becoming crunchy on the outside while remaining soft in the middle.

nut free   gluten free   vegan   soya free   yeast free

Serves 4 as an accompaniment

6 tbsp rapeseed oil
   or olive oil
1 tsp smoked paprika
1 tsp sea salt flakes
4–6 large floury potatoes

Preheat the oven to 200°C (400°F), gas mark 6.

Pour the rapeseed or olive oil into a large mixing bowl, add the paprika and salt and stir together. Slice each potato in half (keeping the skin on), then cut each half lengthways into 4–6 wedges.

Bring a large saucepan of salted water to the boil and blanch the potatoes for 4 minutes. Drain the potatoes and place in the bowl with the oil and spice mixture. Mix thoroughly but carefully, ensuring that each wedge is well coated but not broken. A little bit of marring on the edges won't matter; this will help the wedges to crisp up.

Arrange the wedges on a large baking tray (use two if necessary) in a single layer, ensuring that they do not overlap each other. Cook in the oven for 40–45 minutes or until crisp and golden, turning the wedges every 15 minutes. Remove from the oven and serve immediately.

roasted tomato
& basil sauce

This is an indispensible basic recipe, packed with flavour and highly versatile. By roasting the tomatoes with sugar, garlic and herbs, you add depth and sweetness to the sauce, making it perfect for pouring over gluten-free pasta or spaghetti or for using as a topping for my Pizza Bread (see page 124). And you can include additional ingredients at whim: capers, olives, sun-dried tomatoes, artichoke hearts, roasted vegetables or crisp pancetta lardons would all make wonderful embellishments. Plum tomatoes (baby or otherwise) are best for the sauce, but if you can't get hold of them, decent on-the-vine varieties will work just as well. Needless to say, this recipe is also ideal for using up any gluts of home-grown tomatoes that you may have. Simply multiply the quantities in the recipe and freeze any sauce that you don't use immediately, defrosting it as needed. The sauce can also be placed in an airtight container and stored in the fridge, where it will keep for up to two days.

nut free *gluten free* *vegan* *soya free* *yeast free*

Serves 4

1.5kg plum or vine-ripened tomatoes
1 fat clove of garlic
1 tsp soft light brown sugar
2 tbsp tomato purée
½ tsp dried oregano
3 tbsp olive oil
1 tbsp lemon juice
Leaves from a small bunch of basil
Sea salt flakes and freshly ground black pepper

Preheat the oven to 200°C (400°F), gas mark 6.

Cut the tomatoes in half and finely slice the garlic into rounds. Place the tomatoes in a large roasting tin, spreading them evenly apart, and then sprinkle over the sliced garlic and sugar. Dollop over the tomato purée, scatter over the oregano and drizzle with the olive oil.

Season well with salt and pepper and roast in the oven for 35–40 minutes or until the tomatoes are just beginning to caramelise at the edges.

Remove the tomatoes from the oven and transfer them and any juices to a food processor. Add the lemon juice, then tear up the basil leaves and add to the mixture before blitzing into a coarse tomato sauce. Season with salt and pepper to taste and serve while hot. Alternatively, set aside and then heat through in a saucepan when ready to use.

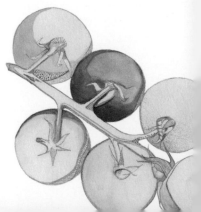

contains nuts

macaroni cheese

Creamy and savoury, yet intolerance friendly, the sauce in this recipe is just close enough to the real deal to remind you of the cheering dish you ate as a child and probably thought you'd never enjoy again. It consists of a white sauce, made with intolerance-friendly ingredients and using toasted and ground pine nuts in place of cheese. Gluten-free macaroni isn't the easiest product to get hold of (see the Glossary, page 230, for stockists of gluten-free pasta), but you can substitute it with gluten-free pasta shells or penne.

contains nuts   *gluten free*   *vegan*   *soya free*   *yeast free*

Serves 4

250g gluten-free macaroni
1 large tomato

For the sauce
150g pine nuts
350ml rice milk
350ml vegetable stock (see the Glossary, page 232)
50g dairy-free margarine
50g gluten-free plain flour (ideally Doves Farm)
Sea salt flakes and freshly ground black pepper

Equipment
You will need a 13cm x 20cm baking dish, about 5cm deep, for this recipe

Preheat the oven to 200°C (400°F), gas mark 6.

First, make the sauce. Scatter the pine nuts on a baking tray and toast in the oven, shaking the tray regularly to ensure they don't catch, for 5–6 minutes or until lightly golden. Remove from the oven (leaving it switched on) and leave to cool. When they have cooled down, place in a food processor and blitz until finely ground.

Pour the rice milk and vegetable stock into a saucepan and heat gently until warm but not simmering. Melt the margarine in another saucepan over a low heat, add the flour and stir vigorously with a wooden spoon to form a roux. Cook for a further 30 seconds, stirring continuously, and then stir in the ground pine nuts.

Gradually pour in the milk and stock, a little at a time and stirring the liquid into the roux as you go, until the sauce is smooth and creamy. Season with salt and pepper to taste and set aside.

Meanwhile, bring a large saucepan of salted water to the boil. Add the macaroni and cook until al dente, following the instructions on the packet – usually 10–12 minutes, though the time may vary according to the brand. Drain the macaroni and then combine with the sauce in one pan, mixing them together well.

Transfer to the baking dish, then slice the tomato into 1cm rounds and layer these over the macaroni. Bake in the oven for 35 minutes or until golden and bubbling.

spaghetti & meatballs

Spaghetti and meatballs provide the perfect easy supper and in my experience are enjoyed by everyone. For my meatballs, I've used a combination of smoked streaky bacon, beef, garlic, herbs and a pinch of mace. The bacon adds flavour, helping to bind the mixture in place of eggs or breadcrumbs and stopping the meatballs from drying out. You can make them in advance and they freeze very well, too.

nut free   gluten free   dairy free   egg free   soya free   yeast free

Serves 4–6

400g gluten-free spaghetti

For the meatballs
2 onions
125g rashers of smoked
    streaky bacon
A small bunch of flat-leaf
    parsley
3 tbsp olive oil
500g minced beef
1 tsp dried oregano
½ tsp mace
2 cloves of garlic
1 x 400g tin of chopped
    tomatoes
1 tbsp lemon juice
100ml chicken stock (see the
    Glossary, page 232)
1 tbsp tomato purée
½ tsp soft light brown sugar
Leaves from a large bunch
    of basil
Sea salt flakes and freshly
    ground black pepper

Finely chop one of the onions until almost minced. Slice the bacon into 3mm lardons and finely chop the parsley. Heat 1 tablespoon of the olive oil in a large frying pan, add the bacon and onion and fry over a low–medium heat for about 10 minutes or until the onion is softened and slightly browned and the bacon has crisped up.

Place the minced beef in a large mixing bowl with the parsley, oregano and mace. Add the fried bacon and onion and season well with salt and pepper. Using your hands, knead the mixture together until well combined and holding its shape.

Take a heaped tablespoon of the mixture and shape into a neat ball, approximately 2.5cm in diameter. Set aside on a plate and continue to shape the rest of the mixture into balls.

Next, chop the remaining onion and crush the garlic. Pour the rest of the oil into the frying pan (used for frying the bacon) and place over a medium heat. When the oil is hot, fry the meatballs (in batches, depending on the size of the pan) for about 5 minutes or until browned and slightly crisp. Use a slotted spoon to scoop them out of the pan, leaving them to rest in a bowl.

Add the remaining onion and the garlic to the pan, then lower the heat and fry gently for about 10 minutes or until soft but not browned. Pour over the tinned tomatoes, lemon juice and stock, then add the tomato purée and sugar. Tear up the basil leaves and add these to the pan, then season with salt and pepper and stir everything together before bringing to a simmer. Add the meatballs to the sauce (juices and all) and simmer gently for 10 minutes.

Meanwhile, bring a large saucepan of salted water to the boil. Add the spaghetti and cook until al dente, following the instructions on the packet – usually 10–12 minutes, depending on the brand. Drain the spaghetti, then combine with the meatballs, mixing them together well before serving.

family favourites

pizza bread

A quick and healthy way of making pizza, the simple dough base and tasty tomato sauce providing the perfect foil for a selection of goodies to go on top. In addition to the items suggested below, you could use roasted peppers, griddled courgettes, fresh spinach, ham, chorizo or sliced salami – the list is endless. The recipe is so easy that it's ideal for making with children; that way, the pleasure of cooking and the choice of topping can be all theirs! This recipe makes one pizza; if you want to make more, simply adjust the quantities for the pizza base and sauce by doubling, tripling and so on, depending on how many you need.

nut free   *gluten free*   *vegan*   *soya free*   *yeast free*

Makes 1 x 20cm pizza

For the pizza base
110g gluten-free self-raising flour (ideally Doves Farm), plus extra for dusting
½ tsp xanthan gum
1 tbsp olive oil, plus extra for greasing
A good pinch of sea salt flakes

For the sauce
1 x 400g tin of chopped tomatoes
1 tbsp tomato purée
1 tsp garlic oil or extra-virgin olive oil
½ tsp lemon juice
½ tsp soft light brown sugar
½ tsp dried oregano
A few basil leaves
Sea salt flakes and freshly ground black pepper

For the topping
Your choice of ingredients (such as chargrilled artichokes, roasted peppers, cooked chicken, olives, raisins, a handful of rocket, a small handful of pine nuts)

First, make the sauce. Drain the juice from the tomatoes, discarding the liquid and placing the tomatoes in a small saucepan. Add the tomato purée, garlic or olive oil, lemon juice, sugar and oregano, season well with salt and pepper and bring to the boil. Lower the heat and leave to simmer for 15 minutes, during which time the sauce will reduce and thicken. Tear up the basil leaves and add to the sauce, then season further to taste and set aside to cool down slightly.

Preheat the oven to 200°C (400°F), gas mark 6, and lightly grease a baking sheet with olive oil.

Sift the flour and xanthan gum into a large mixing bowl, add the olive oil, 4–6 tablespoons of warm water and the salt. Mix together into a stiff dough, adding a little more warm water if the mixture is not coming together – although bear in mind that it shouldn't be too sticky. Pull the dough together with your hands and knead lightly, just stretching it a little to allow the xanthan gum to bind the gluten-free mixture and make it more elastic. Shape the dough into a smooth ball.

Scatter your work surface and rolling pin with a little flour, then transfer the dough from the mixing bowl and roll into a circle approximately 20cm in diameter and 5mm thick, turning up the edges slightly with your fingers to form a crust.

Transfer the pizza base to the prepared baking sheet, then spread over the tomato sauce and layer over your chosen toppings. Place in the oven and bake for 15–20 minutes or until the base is crisp and slightly browned. Serve immediately.

family favourites

creamy garlic, herb & crispy bacon stuffed potatoes

contains nuts

Creamy garlic and herb 'cheese' (see page 56) and crispy smoked bacon transform a humble baked potato into something much more indulgent. Reminiscent of crispy potato skins with sour cream and bacon, these stuffed potatoes are even tastier, I think, and have far less fat. Just right for a cosy evening in, with a fresh green salad on the side.

contains nuts   *gluten free*   *dairy free*   *egg free*   *soya free*   *yeast free*

Serves 4

4 x 400g floury potatoes (such as Maris Piper, King Edward or Golden Wonder)
100g smoked streaky bacon
4 tbsp Garlic and Herb Cashew Cream Cheese (see page 56)
A small bunch of chives

Preheat the oven to 200°C (400°F), gas mark 6.

Prick the potatoes all over with a fork or a small sharp knife. Place on the middle shelf of the oven and bake for 45–60 minutes, depending on the size of the potatoes. They are done when the flesh gives a little when you squeeze them gently between your thumb and forefinger. Remove from the oven, leaving it switched on, and set aside to cool for 5 minutes.

While the potatoes are baking, finely slice the bacon into 1cm lardons. Heat a non-stick frying pan and dry-fry the bacon over a medium heat for 7–8 minutes or until crisp and golden.

Slice the baked potatoes in half, scoop out the flesh with a teaspoon and place in a bowl. Add the Garlic and Herb Cashew Cream Cheese and the bacon and mash together with a fork. Spoon the filling back into the potato skins, place on a baking tray and return to the oven for a further 15 minutes.

Remove from the oven, then finely chop the chives and sprinkle them over the potatoes before serving.

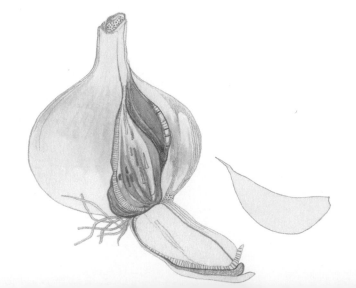

Like macaroni cheese (see page 121), shepherd's pie is another nursery favourite and a sure winner for a hearty family supper. This particular version is true to its classic roots: minced lamb, carrots, peas and a few herbs make up the body of the dish, while the topping is pure, creamy mashed potato. You could ring the changes by substituting half of the potatoes with sweet potato; its golden flesh goes really well with the lamb. Don't underestimate the power of a good shepherd's pie – it's pure comfort food with the advantage of being naturally allergen free. Serve with your favourite selection of vegetables – steamed broccoli, extra peas and roast parsnips always make my list. If you want to make this in advance, it freezes very well. Just leave to defrost overnight and then cook it for the full 25 minutes when you want to serve it.

nut free   gluten free   dairy free   egg free   soya free   yeast free

Serves 4–6

1 large onion
2 carrots
700g floury potatoes (ideally King Edward or Maris Piper)
450g lean minced lamb
1 bouquet garni
150g fresh or frozen peas
300ml vegetable stock (see the Glossary, page 232)
1 tbsp tomato purée
1 tsp cornflour mixed with 1 tbsp warm water
2 tbsp good-quality olive oil
Sea salt flakes and freshly ground black pepper

Equipment
You will need an ovenproof pie dish measuring about 20cm x 28cm for this recipe

Roughly chop the onion, then trim and peel the carrots and cut into 1cm dice. Peel the potatoes, cut into 5cm chunks and place in a large saucepan of salted water, ready to cook.

Heat a large non-stick frying pan and dry-fry the minced lamb over a medium heat for 2 minutes, breaking it up a little with a wooden spoon so that it doesn't clump together. Add the chopped onion and carrots to the pan with the bouquet garni and peas and continue to fry, stirring frequently, for 8–10 minutes or until the onion and carrots are starting to soften.

Pour over the stock, season well with salt and pepper and add the tomato purée. Stir to combine and then gradually add the cornflour mixture, stirring gently all the while, until the meat has absorbed half of the stock and thickened up noticeably. Cover the pan with a lid and simmer gently over a low heat for a further 25 minutes.

While the mince is cooking, bring the saucepan containing the potatoes to the boil and cook for 15–20 minutes or until tender to the point of a knife. Drain the potatoes, return them to their pan, season well with salt and pepper and add the olive oil. Mash well until smooth and creamy.

While the potatoes are cooking, preheat the oven to 200°C (400°F), gas mark 6.

Spoon the lamb mixture into the pie dish and carefully cover with the mashed potato. (The easiest way is spoonful by spoonful, working from the outside in a spiral to the centre of the dish.) Run the back of a fork over the potato topping and then bake in the oven for 20–25 minutes or until golden brown and bubbling on top.

fish pie

Fish pie is the ultimate comfort food: delicately flavoured yet hearty enough for a winter's day and sufficiently robust to satisfy the largest of appetites. I've added a gentle twist by including parsley in the sauce, effectively making it a parsley sauce, which I think goes brilliantly with the fish. Serve with a bowlful of garden peas for a delicious family supper.

nut free   *gluten free*   *dairy free*   *egg free*   *soya free*   *yeast free*

Serves 4

1 white onion
300g smoked haddock
300g cod or other white fish fillets
750ml rice milk
1 bay leaf
110g dairy-free margarine, plus extra for dotting on top
60g gluten-free plain flour (ideally Doves Farm)
A small bunch of curly-leaf parsley
1kg floury potatoes (preferably Maris Piper)
Sea salt flakes and freshly ground black pepper

Equipment
You will need a 20cm round ovenproof pie dish for this recipe

Preheat the oven to 200°C (400°F), gas mark 6.

Finely chop the onion and put in a shallow saucepan with the fish and the rice milk. Add the bay leaf and season with black pepper. Bring to the boil, then reduce the heat and simmer gently for 3 minutes. (You may find that the rice milk separates a little, but this is nothing to worry about.) Remove from the heat, cover the pan with a lid or plate and leave to cool.

Lift the fish and bay leaf out of the rice milk using a slotted spoon and place on a plate. Remove the skin and any bones, then flake the fish, keeping it in reasonable-sized pieces, and set aside while you make the sauce.

In a large saucepan, melt 60g of the margarine over a medium heat and then add the flour. Stir together to form a roux and cook, stirring continuously, for 1 minute. Pour over 500ml of the poaching milk and stir rapidly with a whisk until all of the liquid has been absorbed and the sauce is smooth.

Finely chop the parsley and add to the sauce with the flaked fish, stirring in gently so as not to break up the pieces of fish. Season with salt and pepper, then leave to cool while you prepare the potatoes.

Peel the potatoes and cut into 2.5cm chunks. Place in a large saucepan of salted water and bring to the boil, then reduce the heat and leave to simmer for 10–15 minutes or until completely soft to the point of a knife. Mash with the remaining margarine and season generously with salt and pepper.

Place the fish mixture in the pie dish and carefully top with the mashed potato. (The easiest way is spoonful by spoonful, working from the outside in a spiral to the centre of the dish.) Run the back of a fork over the surface and dot with a little extra margarine, then place in the oven to bake for 45 minutes or until bubbling and golden on top.

bang bang chicken

Bang bang chicken is a classic Indonesian dish of finely sliced vegetables topped with cooked chicken and a peanut sauce. Using sunflower seeds in place of the traditional peanut butter, my version is nut free, making it perfect for everyone. It also goes down very well with children. Serve with a portion of steamed basmati rice for a colourful, light yet satisfying supper.

nut free   *gluten free*   *dairy free*   *egg free*   *soya free*   *yeast free*

Serves 4

A small bunch of coriander
Juice of 1 lime (reserving
   1 tbsp for the sauce)
4 skinless chicken breasts
4 carrots
½ cucumber

For the bang bang sauce
75g sunflower seeds
2 tbsp rapeseed or olive oil
¼ fresh red chilli (deseeded)
1 tbsp reserved lime juice
1 tbsp tamarind paste
1 tbsp maple syrup

Chop the stalks from the coriander (reserving the leaves for later) and place in a large saucepan filled three-quarters with water. Add the lime juice and bring to the boil. Once the water is boiling, place the chicken breasts in the pan and cover with a lid, then remove from the heat and leave to stand for 50–60 minutes. Drain the chicken, discarding the coriander stalks, and pat dry on kitchen paper.

While the chicken is poaching, preheat the oven to 180°C (350°F), gas mark 4, and make the sauce.

Scatter the sunflower seeds over a baking tray and toast in the oven, shaking the tray every now and then to make sure they don't burn, for 5–6 minutes or until lightly golden. Remove from the oven and set aside to cool down. When the seeds are cool, place in a food processor and pulse into a powder the consistency of very fine breadcrumbs. Keep blitzing the seeds and start to add the rapeseed or olive oil, bit by bit, until you have a creamy sunflower seed butter.

Finely chop the red chilli and add to the sunflower seed butter with the reserved tablespoon of lime juice, the tamarind paste and maple syrup. Blitz in the food processor until combined, then add 4–5 tablespoons of water to the mixture, a little at a time as you continue blitzing, until you have a sauce that is thick but of pouring consistency. Transfer to a bowl, cover with cling film and leave out until ready to serve – if you refrigerate the sauce, it tends to thicken up considerably.

When ready to serve, peel both the carrots and the cucumber and then – using a very sharp knife, wide vegetable peeler or mandolin – slice lengthways into thin ribbons. Pile the vegetable ribbons onto a serving platter and, using your hands, shred the poached chicken over the top. Pour over the bang bang sauce and scatter over the reserved coriander leaves to serve.

marmalade-baked
chicken
creamy chicken,
herb & mushroom penne
seared chicken breasts
with spiced coconut rice
prawn & chorizo spaghetti
baked italian
chicken & rice
creamy chicken curry

WEEKNIGHT food

moroccan
vegetable tagine
roast pork with potatoes,
lemon, fennel & capers
whole roast jerk chicken
chicken, artichoke
& caper stew
sweet chilli
& sesame salmon

marmalade-baked chicken

You may be wondering about the combination of marmalade and chicken, but once you've tasted this you'll realise it's the perfect match, especially when cooked, as here, with tomatoes and roasted sweet potato. This dish has the added benefit of being effortless to put together, making it an ideal midweek supper. Serve with a bowl of basmati rice and some fresh steamed greens or broccoli for a feast of flavour and vibrant colour.

nut free   *gluten free*   *dairy free*   *egg free*   *soya free*   *yeast free*

Serves 4

1 sweet potato
1 large white onion
2 sticks of celery
1 fat clove of garlic
4 skinless chicken breasts
2 tbsp olive oil
1 x 400g tin of chopped
   tomatoes
3 tbsp marmalade
1 tbsp lemon juice
½ tbsp tomato purée
Leaves from 6 oregano
   stems
Sea salt flakes and freshly
   ground black pepper

Preheat the oven to 180°C (350°F), gas mark 4.

Peel the sweet potato and chop into 2.5cm chunks. Finely chop the onion and celery, crush the garlic and slice the chicken into cubes the same size as the sweet potato pieces.

Heat the olive oil in a heavy-based ovenproof frying pan or casserole dish. When the oil is hot, fry the chicken over a medium heat for 5–6 minutes or until lightly browned on each side and then scoop out with a slotted spoon and set aside. Add the onion to the pan or dish with the celery, garlic and sweet potato and fry over a low heat for 10 minutes or until the onion has softened and all the vegetables are lightly golden.

Return the chicken to the pan, pour over the tinned tomatoes and then stir in the marmalade, lemon juice, tomato purée and oregano. Season generously with salt and pepper and transfer to the oven, leaving to cook, uncovered, for 40 minutes or until the chicken is cooked though but tender and the sauce is bubbling and thick.

creamy chicken, herb & mushroom penne

contains nuts

Fast, simple and incredibly scrumptious, this pasta dish is just the thing for a midweek supper. Gluten-free penne (or your choice of pasta), tender chicken and sautéed mushrooms are mixed with my Garlic and Herb Cashew Cream Cheese (see page 56), adding a real touch of decadence to the dish. Topped with slices of sun-dried tomato, this would be delicious served with a green leafy salad and perhaps some Focaccia (see page 180) on the side.

contains nuts   *gluten free*   *dairy free*   *egg free*   *soya free*   *yeast free*

Serves 4

1 large onion
250g chestnut mushrooms
4 sun-dried tomatoes
2 chicken breasts
2–3 tbsp olive oil
400g gluten-free penne
300g Garlic and Herb
    Cashew Cream Cheese
    (see page 56)
Sea salt flakes and freshly
    ground black pepper

Finely chop the onion and finely slice mushrooms and sun-dried tomatoes. Slice the chicken breasts in half horizontally, so that you have four flat fillets of the same size, and season well on both sides with salt and pepper.

Heat 2 tablespoons of olive oil in a heavy-based frying pan and when it is hot, add the chicken and fry on each side over a medium heat for 3 minutes or until lightly golden and cooked through. Remove from the pan, leave to rest for 5 minutes and then cut into 5mm-thick slices.

Add the onion and mushrooms to the pan, using more oil if needed, and fry over a low heat for 15–20 minutes or until completely soft.

Meanwhile, bring a large saucepan of salted water to the boil, add the penne and cook until al dente, following the instructions on the packet – usually 10–12 minutes, depending on the brand of pasta.

Drain the penne and tip into the pan with the mushrooms and onion, add the cooked chicken and the Garlic and Herb Cashew Cream Cheese and stir together over a low heat until the cream cheese has coated the pasta and is warmed through. Spoon into bowls, scatter over the sliced sun-dried tomatoes and serve immediately.

seared chicken breasts with spiced coconut rice

Just the sort of thing to warm you, body and soul, on a cold wintry day, this delicious dish uses the simplest of ingredients to create a hearty and fragrantly spiced meal. Serve with a light tomato chutney or simply enjoy on its own and allow its comforting flavours to soothe you. You can make it using my simple curry paste – which would also make the perfect base for vegetable or other curries – or a ready-made one of your choice; just ensure that it doesn't contain any allergens.

contains nuts   *nut-free option*   *gluten free*   *dairy free*   *egg free*   *soya free*   *yeast free*

Serves 4

1 tbsp olive oil
200g white basmati rice
250ml full-fat coconut milk
300ml chicken stock (see the Glossary, page 232)
4 chicken breasts (skin left on)
2 tbsp sunflower or rapeseed oil
Sea salt flakes and freshly ground black pepper

For the curry paste
2 tomatoes
1 fresh red chilli
1 clove of garlic
1cm piece of root ginger
A large bunch of coriander
Juice of 1 lemon
½ tsp mustard seeds
1 tsp toasted sesame oil (omit for a nut-free option)

First, make the curry paste. Halve the tomatoes and chilli pepper (removing the seeds if you don't want the paste to be too hot) and place in a food processor. Add the garlic, ginger and coriander (reserving a few stems for adding at the end), then blitz until finely chopped. Alternatively, finely chop all these ingredients by hand until almost minced. Stir in the lemon juice, mustard seeds and sesame oil (if using). (The paste may appear quite liquid, but this is normal and there's no need to worry about it.)

Heat the olive oil in a large saucepan, add the curry paste and cook over a medium heat for a couple of minutes. Stir in the rice and continue to cook for 2–3 minutes or until the rice is glassy in appearance. Pour over the coconut milk and chicken stock, bring to the boil and then simmer for 15–20 minutes or until the rice is just cooked.

Meanwhile, rinse the chicken breasts and pat dry on kitchen paper, then season generously with salt and pepper. Heat the sunflower or rapeseed oil in a large frying pan over a medium-high heat. When the oil is hot, add the chicken breasts, skin-side down, and fry for 5 minutes before turning over and frying for a further 4 minutes or until cooked through. Remove from the pan and leave to rest for 5 minutes before slicing on the diagonal into 1cm strips.

Spoon the rice into four large bowls, placing the sliced chicken on top. Finely chop the remaining coriander and scatter over the top to finish.

prawn &
chorizo spaghetti

If you've already made the Roasted Tomato and Basil Sauce (see page 120), then this simple dish is ultra-quick to prepare – ideal for a midweek supper. The mix of smoky, salty chorizo and sweet prawns creates the most seductive combination of flavours, but if you like things a bit spicier, you can always add a pinch of chilli flakes to the mix. Be sure to check the ingredients of the chorizo to make sure it contains only pork and seasonings and no allergenic ingredients (see the Glossary, page 226, for recommended suppliers).

nut free   *gluten free*   *dairy free*   *egg free*   *soya free*   *yeast free*

Serves 4–6

150g chorizo
A small bunch of flat-leaf
    parsley
400g gluten-free spaghetti
150g raw tiger prawns
    (peeled and deveined)
1 portion of Roasted Tomato
    and Basil Sauce (see
    page 120)
Sea salt flakes

Slice the chorizo into 1cm dice, then finely chop the parsley and set aside.

Bring a large saucepan of salted water to the boil, add the spaghetti and cook – stirring occasionally to stop the spaghetti sticking – until al dente, following the instructions on the packet – usually 10–12 minutes depending on the brand of pasta. Drain and return the spaghetti to the pan.

Meanwhile, place a frying pan over a medium heat and when it is hot, add the diced chorizo and dry-fry for a minute or two or until just starting to crisp and release its oils. Add the prawns and fry for a further 2–3 minutes or until cooked through.

Add the Roasted Tomato and Basil Sauce to the prawns and chorizo in the pan and heat through. Pour the finished sauce over the cooked spaghetti, then stir together and spoon into bowls before scattering over the chopped parsley to serve.

baked italian chicken & rice

This recipe is so easy to put together and has the benefit of being a one-pot meal, making it quick to prepare and brilliant for sharing – just plonk it on the table and dish up! Although not the traditional way of cooking risotto, the layering of rice and chicken ensures the meat stays tender and moist, while the rice benefits by absorbing all the juices. Don't worry if at the end of cooking the rice is still slightly wet – like any good risotto, this dish shouldn't be dry but should retain a light, glaze-like sauce.

nut free   gluten free   dairy free   egg free   soya free   yeast free

Serves 4

2 skinless chicken breasts
200g smoked streaky bacon
1 large onion
1 fennel bulb
4 large vine tomatoes
2 cloves of garlic
A small bunch of basil
A small bunch of marjoram
2 tbsp olive oil, plus extra
    for greasing
175g Arborio rice
½ tsp dried oregano
50g pitted black olives
500ml chicken stock (see the
    Glossary, page 232)
Sea salt flakes and freshly
    ground black pepper

Preheat the oven to 180°C (350°F), gas mark 4, and lightly grease a heavy-based casserole dish with olive oil.

Cut the chicken breasts into 5cm chunks and slice the bacon into small lardons. Halve the onion and slice into thin half-moons. Trim the ends from the fennel bulb, cut into quarters lengthways and then into 1cm dice. Chop the tomatoes into large chunks roughly the same size as the chicken pieces. Crush the garlic and finely chop the fresh herbs.

Heat half the olive oil in the casserole dish and fry the bacon lardons over a medium heat for about 5 minutes or until golden at the edges and slightly crisp. Use a slotted spoon to scoop the lardons out of the pan and transfer them to a large mixing bowl. Add the chicken to the casserole dish and fry for 3–4 minutes or until sealed and lightly golden. Set aside to rest.

Reduce the heat and pour the remaining olive oil into the dish. Add the fennel, onion and garlic, season well with salt and pepper and fry gently for about 15 minutes or until softened. Transfer the cooked onion, fennel and garlic to the mixing bowl, add the uncooked rice with the oregano, olives, chopped fresh herbs and tomatoes, then stir together until combined.

Spoon half of the rice mixture back into the casserole dish and then layer the chicken over the top. Cover with the remaining rice, pour over the stock, then cover with the lid and bake in the oven for 55 minutes (removing the lid for the last 5 minutes of cooking time) or until the chicken is cooked through and most of the liquid has been absorbed.

creamy
chicken curry

This is one of easiest of curries to make: with a little prep, a bit of marinating and a blast of oven-baking, you have a rich and fragrant dish that does more, I think, for body and soul after a long day than pretty much anything else. I've chosen to use chicken thighs because I think they have the best flavour, but feel free to use whatever cut, or indeed meat, you like. The spices are a simple blend and are in no way gospel: use whatever you have and miss out what you don't have. That's the beauty of making a curry – you can ramp the spices up or down entirely to suit you. I recommend this combination of spices, however, and I think the coconut milk is key, adding creaminess and a buttery note. Serve with basmati rice, lots of fresh coriander and a poppadom or two.

nut free *gluten free* *dairy free* *egg free* *soya free* *yeast free*

Serves 4

8 skinless and boneless
    chicken thighs
2 cloves of garlic
1 large white onion
2 tbsp sunflower or
    rapeseed oil
Leaves from a small bunch
    of coriander
Sea salt flakes and freshly
    ground black pepper

For the marinade
1 x 400ml tin of full-fat
    coconut milk
Juice of ½ lemon
½ tsp black mustard seeds
1 tsp garam masala
2 tsp smoked paprika
2 tsp ground coriander
1 tsp ground cumin
½ tsp turmeric
½–1 tsp chilli powder
    (or to taste)
¼ tsp ground ginger

First, prepare the marinade. Place the coconut milk and lemon juice in a large mixing bowl, add the spices and stir together until blended. Make a few diagonal cuts, about 1cm deep, in each chicken thigh and then add to the marinade, leaving to marinate for 2–24 hours. If marinating for longer than 2 hours, place the chicken in the fridge, removing it and allowing it to come to room temperature before cooking.

Preheat the oven to 220°C (425°F), gas mark 7.

Finely slice the garlic and halve the onion and cut into thin half-moons. Heat the sunflower or rapeseed oil in a shallow heavy-based casserole dish, then fry the onion and garlic over a medium heat for 5–10 minutes or until softened and just starting to brown.

Add the chicken thighs and marinade to the casserole dish, season well with salt and pepper and then bake in the oven for 30–35 minutes or until bubbling and fragrant and the chicken is cooked through. Serve on a bed of basmati rice with a scattering of torn coriander leaves over the top.

moroccan
vegetable tagine

What could be more sumptuous on a wintry day than this slow-cooked tagine, packed with vegetables and aromatic with spices? The spice mixture given here is really just a guideline – feel free to add to or subtract from it as you wish. If you don't like a certain spice, just leave it out. You can ring the changes with the vegetables, too: parsnips, sweet potato and courgettes would all work equally well. This is really about the overall effect of the dish rather than the individual elements. Serve it with a big bowl of brown rice and some steamed broccoli – it's sure to warm you up!

nut free   gluten free   vegan   soya free   yeast free

Serves 4–6

2 large red onions
2 cloves of garlic
1 fennel bulb
1 large butternut squash
1 large aubergine
1 tbsp olive oil
1 x 400g tin of chopped
    tomatoes
1 tbsp tomato purée

For the spice mixture
Seeds of 1 cardamom pod
½ tsp coriander seeds
½ tsp allspice berries
½ tsp ground ginger
1 tsp smoked paprika
½ tsp ground mace
½ tsp turmeric
½ tsp cayenne pepper
½ tsp chilli flakes
½ tsp sea salt flakes
½ tsp freshly ground
    black pepper
2 tbsp olive oil
1 tbsp runny honey

Preheat the oven to 130°C (250°F), gas mark ½.

First, prepare the spice mixture. Place the cardamom seeds, coriander seeds and allspice berries in a small heavy-based frying pan and dry-fry over a medium heat until you can smell their aroma – about 1 minute, but keep an eye on them to make sure they don't burn. Transfer to a mortar and grind to a fine powder with a pestle. Alternatively, place in a freezer bag and crush with a rolling pin.

Next, combine all of the spices together in a small bowl. Pour over the olive oil and honey and stir together until combined.

Halve the onions and cut into half-moon slices, then slice the garlic into thin rounds. Trim the fennel and peel and halve the butternut squash, scooping out the pith and seeds. Chop the fennel, squash and aubergine into large chunks approximately 4cm in size.

Heat the olive oil in a large heavy-based casserole dish. When the oil is hot, gently fry the onion and garlic over a low–medium heat for 10 minutes or until softened. Add the squash and fry for a further 10 minutes or until it begins to give at the edges. Add the fennel and aubergine to the dish and stir everything together.

Pour over the spice mixture and stir in until evenly mixed, frying for a further minute. Add the chopped tomatoes and tomato purée, bring to a rolling simmer and then cover with a lid and transfer to the oven to cook for 2½–3 hours until the vegetables are soft and melding together.

roast pork with potatoes, lemon, fennel & capers

This is a wonderfully simple dish, effortless to prepare and hence ideal for serving to friends and family at the end of a busy day. By baking everything together, you collect all of the wonderful juices and flavours in the bottom of the tin: fragrant juniper, tangy lemon, piquant capers and aromatic fennel all linger to make an intense and delightful sauce. It complements the tender pork to perfection, while the roast potatoes add body and texture to the dish. Serve with a bowl of steamed green beans or perhaps some roasted peppers.

nut free   gluten free   dairy free   egg free   soya free   yeast free

Serves 4

4 juniper berries
1 tbsp demerara sugar
Grated zest and juice of
 1 lemon
1 x 500g pork tenderloin
4 tbsp olive oil
4 large floury potatoes
 (such as Maris Piper, Lady
 Balfour or King Edward)
2 fennel bulbs
1 tbsp capers, drained
 and rinsed
250ml hot vegetable stock
 (see the Glossary, page
 232) or water
1 tsp cornflour mixed with
 1 tsp water
Sea salt flakes and freshly
 ground black pepper

Preheat the oven to 180°C (350°F), gas mark 4.

Using a pestle and mortar, crush the juniper berries into a fine powder. (Alternatively, place in a freezer bag and crush with a rolling pin.) Transfer to a small bowl and stir in the demerara sugar and lemon zest. Lay the pork tenderloin flat on a plate, rub over 1 tablespoon of the olive oil and season with salt and pepper. Scatter over the sugar, lemon and juniper mix and set aside at room temperature.

Cut the potatoes (no need to peel) into 1cm-thick slices. Trim the ends from the fennel bulbs and cut lengthways into slices the same thickness as the potatoes. Pour the remaining olive oil into a large roasting tin, then spread the fennel slices over the base of the tin, layer over the potato slices and season well with salt and pepper.

Roast in the oven for 40 minutes, giving the tin a shake every now and then to stop the vegetables catching. Place the marinated pork on top of the potatoes, scatter over the capers and drizzle over the lemon juice. Return to the oven for 25–30 minutes or until the meat is tender and cooked through.

Remove from the oven and transfer the potatoes, fennel and pork to a warm serving dish, cover with foil and rest for 10 minutes. Meanwhile, place the roasting tin over a low heat and pour in the hot stock or water. Bring to a simmer, scraping up any caramelised bits stuck to the base of the pan, then lower the heat, pour in the cornflour mixture and whisk until you have a smooth and light gravy.

Slice the pork into 1cm wedges and serve with the fennel, potatoes and a pouring of the gravy.

whole roast jerk chicken

This recipe was born from my love of roast chicken. What other dish evokes such positive associations? The warmth of Sunday lunch with the family; the treat of a chicken sandwich made with delicious leftovers; the comfort of chicken soup prepared with fresh stock; the cheer of a chicken pie with mashed-potato topping after a long day out in the cold. Roast chicken represents, to me, what cooking is all about: the sheer pleasure that comes from making simple yet delicious dishes and sharing them with friends and family. The best roast chicken is made by slathering the skin in butter before roasting – it helps to brown the skin and creates a wonderful creaminess to the meat. Here, I've used a natural alternative to butter, coconut oil, to recreate that seductive flavour. The taste of the coconut marries wonderfully with the various spices to produce a heavenly twist on a simple roast chicken, while the combination of roasted sweet potato and peppers adds to the vibrancy of the dish. It's best served with a crisp green salad, the crunch adding vital contrast. If you want a slightly larger spread, then add a bowl of cooked rice and a good tomato chutney (ideally freshly made with coriander) to give the right sweet/spicy balance.

nut free   gluten free   dairy free   egg free   soya free   yeast free

Serves 4

1 x 1.8kg chicken
1 lemon
2 large sweet potatoes
2 red peppers
2 red onions
Sea salt flakes and freshly
   ground black pepper

For the jerk spice mixture
1cm piece of root ginger
2 cloves of garlic
2 tsp soft light brown sugar
1 tsp dried thyme
1 tsp fennel seeds
1 tsp caraway seeds
½ tbsp ground coriander
1 tsp ground ginger
1 tsp smoked paprika
1 tsp ground cinnamon
1 tsp ground allspice
1 tsp chilli flakes (or to taste)
100g coconut oil (in a solid
   state at room
   temperature)

Preheat the oven to 230°C (450°F), gas mark 8.

First, prepare the jerk spice mixture. Finely grate the ginger and crush the garlic, then add to a mixing bowl with all the remaining ingredients for the spice mixture. Add the coconut oil and stir in until evenly blended.

Place the chicken in a roasting tin and smear all of the spiced coconut oil over the skin. Season generously with salt and pepper and then cut the lemon in half and squeeze the juice over the bird before stuffing the cavity with the used lemon halves.

Next, peel the sweet potatoes and cut into 8cm wedges. Remove the stalks and seeds from the peppers and cut the flesh into 2.5cm-wide lengths, then slice the onions into quarters lengthways.

Place the chicken in the oven to roast for 10–15 minutes, then reduce the temperature to 190°C (375°F), gas mark 5. Remove from the oven and add the sweet potatoes, peppers and onions to the tin before roasting for a further 35–40 minutes or until the skin of the chicken is crisp and golden and the juices run clear when tested with a knife.

continues...

weeknight food

Remove from the oven, cover the tin with foil and leave to rest for 10 minutes before carving the chicken.

Serve the chicken on a bed of sweet potatoes, red peppers and softened onion.

Use up any leftover chicken by making a Chicken and Mango Salad: tear up the remaining chicken and toss together with a diced ripe mango, shredded chinese lettuce, fresh coriander, finely chopped red chilli, toasted cashew nuts and a squeeze of lemon juice...

chicken, artichoke & caper stew

This light and zesty stew always makes me think of spring, although you could eat it at any time, as it uses ingredients that are available all year round. The sauce is fresh and fragrant thanks to the inclusion of lemon juice, capers and herbs. The whole dish offers all the heartiness and warmth of a proper stew without any of the heaviness – perfect for a weekday supper. You can serve it as it is, the potatoes giving enough body to the dish, or, for a more substantial meal, serve with caraway-roasted carrots and some basmati rice to soak up all the juices.

nut free   gluten free   dairy free   egg free   soya free   yeast free

Serves 4–6

400g new potatoes
2 large white onions
5 cloves of garlic
150g artichoke hearts in olive oil, drained (retaining the oil for frying if you like)
A small bunch of flat-leaf parsley
A small bunch of chives
2 skinless chicken breasts
6 skinless and boneless chicken thighs
3 tbsp olive oil (or use the oil drained from the artichokes)
500ml chicken or vegetable stock (see the Glossary, page 232)
2 tbsp capers, drained and rinsed
Juice of 1 lemon
100ml rice milk
1 tsp cornflour mixed with 1 tbsp rice milk
Sea salt flakes and freshly ground black pepper

Scrub the potatoes, if necessary, and cut into halves or quarters depending on their size – you want them to be in small bite-sized chunks. Roughly chop the onions and crush the garlic. Cut the artichoke hearts into halves (if not halved already in the jar) and finely chop the fresh herbs. Slice each chicken breast diagonally in half and then season all the chicken generously with salt and pepper.

Pour the olive oil into a large heavy-based casserole dish and place over a medium-high heat. When the oil is hot, add the chicken pieces and fry on each side until sealed and golden – around 5 minutes in total. Use a slotted spoon to remove the chicken from the pan and set aside. Add the onions and garlic to the casserole dish, then reduce the heat and fry gently for about 5 minutes or until starting to soften.

Add the potatoes to the dish and fry for a further minute or so. Turn up the heat slightly, then return the chicken to the pan and pour over the stock. Bring to the boil, then reduce to a simmer and leave to bubble away, uncovered, for 25–30 minutes or until the potatoes are tender and the chicken cooked through.

Add the artichokes to the dish with the capers, lemon juice, rice milk and cornflour mixture. Stir everything together and allow to simmer gently for 2–3 minutes or until the sauce has thickened slightly. Add the fresh herbs to the dish, stir in and then season with salt and pepper to taste before serving.

sweet chilli
& sesame salmon

nut–free
option

I love to make my own sweet chilli sauce, using a combination of sugar, maple syrup, lime, chilli and fish sauce. Not only does it have a real depth of flavour, and enough colour to brighten up the most abject of evenings, but it is gloriously simple to make and much better for you than any bought variety. It delivers a sweet–spicy kick that offsets the rich oiliness of salmon, but it would work equally well with other types of fish and meat – I often serve it with seared prawns, chicken and even pork – or added to stir–fries. The sesame seed crust on the salmon adds to the overall texture with its mellow bite, complemented in turn by the sharp crunch of the spring onions. For me, there is only one way to serve this dish and that is on a bed of light and fluffy basmati rice. A twist of fresh lime and some lightly steamed broccoli are all it needs to make it into a sumptuous meal.

contains nuts   nut-free option   gluten free   dairy free   egg free   soya free   yeast free

Serves 4

4 x 180g salmon fillets
1 tbsp toasted sesame oil
    (or smoked rapeseed oil
    for a nut-free option)
1 tbsp sesame seeds (or omit
    for a nut-free option)
3 spring onions
Sea salt flakes and freshly
    ground black pepper

For the sweet chilli sauce
2 tbsp maple syrup
2 tbsp soft dark brown sugar
1 fresh red chilli
2 tbsp lime juice
2 tbsp fish sauce
A small bunch of coriander

Begin by making the sauce. Place the maple syrup and brown sugar in a small saucepan, add 2 tablespoons of water and heat gently until the sugar has dissolved. Finely chop the chilli and tip into the pan (seeds and all), then continue to cook over a medium heat for around 5 minutes or until you have a pale gold sauce speckled with the chilli.

Remove from the heat and stir in the lime juice and fish sauce, then finely chop the coriander and add to the pan. Taste the sauce, adding a little extra lime juice if necessary.

Preheat the grill to high and line the grill pan or a baking sheet with foil.

Place the salmon fillets in the lined grill pan or on the baking sheet and lightly brush with the toasted sesame oil (or smoked rapeseed oil). Season with salt and pepper and then sprinkle the sesame seeds (if using) evenly over the fillets. Place under the grill and cook for around 7 minutes or until the salmon is cooked through but still tender and moist.

Remove from the grill, place on individual plates and pour over the sweet chilli sauce. Finely chop the spring onions and sprinkle over to serve.

chilli con carne
cornbread
sausage, lentil &
sun-dried tomato cassoulet
masala chicken
dhal with
caraway aubergine
sweet potato &
onion bhaji bites
baby squash with
leeks & gorgonzola & herb cheese
baked
preserved lemon tagine
creamy caponata bake
chestnut & chorizo stew
lamb, apricot
& tahini meatballs
chickpea pancakes
butter bean
hummus with mint oil

Fireside suppers

chilli
con carne

Chilli con carne is such a classic dish. Simple to make and comforting to eat, it's the perfect thing to serve for a family supper or a heartening meal on a cold winter's day. It also lends itself to being easily adapted – a little gluten-free flour is all that's needed – but it's the addition of coffee and a little dark chocolate that elevates this recipe. The flavours become deeper, more fragrant and intensely rich. Serve with Cornbread (see page 156), basmati rice and some crisp, finely shredded iceberg lettuce, and for best results make the day before, leaving the flavours to really develop.

nut free   *gluten free*   *dairy free*   *egg free*   *soya free*   *yeast free*

Serves 4

2 onions
2 fresh red chillies
3 cloves of garlic
1kg braising steak
1 tbsp rice or gram flour
3 tbsp olive oil
1 x 400g tin of chopped tomatoes
1 x 400g tin of kidney beans, drained and rinsed (optional)
1 tbsp tomato purée
½ tsp chilli powder (or to taste)
¼ tsp ground cinnamon
1 tsp soft light brown sugar
300ml beef stock
200ml freshly made coffee
15g dairy- and soya-free dark chocolate (2–4 squares in total)
Sea salt flakes and freshly ground black pepper

Preheat the oven to 170°C (325°F), gas mark 3.

Roughly chop the onions and finely slice the chillies, keeping the seeds. Crush the garlic and dice the beef into 2cm cubes.

Place the flour in a large mixing bowl, season generously with salt and pepper and then add the cubed beef, tossing with your hands until lightly coated in the flour. Heat half the olive oil in a large, heavy-based casserole dish, add half the beef and fry over a medium–high heat for 5–6 minutes or until browned on all sides. Use a slotted spoon to transfer the beef to a plate, then fry the rest of the meat in the remaining olive oil before transferring to the plate with the first batch of beef.

Next, add the onions to the dish and fry over a medium heat for 5–10 minutes or until soft and just starting to brown. Add the garlic and chillies and cook for another minute or so.

Return the beef to the casserole dish along with the chopped tomatoes, kidney beans (if using), tomato purée, chilli powder, cinnamon, sugar, stock and coffee. Bring to the boil, then cover with a lid and transfer to the oven to cook gently for 1½ hours or until the beef is tender and the sauce thick and fragrant. When ready, remove from the oven and stir in the chocolate until melted and fully incorporated.

cornbread

Traditionally made from ground corn, leavened with baking powder and fried in a deep skillet, cornbread hails from America where it has long been a staple accompaniment to any meal. My particular version is baked in a tin and uses corn in the guise of polenta, with creamed corn acting in place of eggs to help bind the mixture together. I love the sweet flavour and golden colour of this bread and can think of no better companion to a good Chilli con Carne (see page 154) or barbecued meal. It's also delicious for breakfast, served with Busy Boston Baked Beans (see page 118) or a few rashers of crisp, smoked streaky bacon and some grilled mushrooms. Once made, it will keep for up to three days if stored in an airtight container.

nut free *gluten free* *vegan* *soya free* *yeast free*

Serves 8

300ml rice milk
2 tbsp lemon juice
125g gluten-free plain flour
    (ideally Doves Farm)
4 tsp gluten-free baking
    powder
175g polenta or cornmeal
1 tbsp golden caster sugar
½ tsp sea salt flakes, plus
    extra for sprinkling
6 heaped tbsp creamed corn
4 tbsp olive oil, plus extra
    for greasing
¼ tsp chilli flakes (optional)

Equipment
You will need an 18cm square
    baking tin for this recipe

In a jug or bowl, whisk together the rice milk and lemon juice and then set aside for 5 minutes so that the lemon can sour the milk.

Preheat the oven to 200°C (400°F), gas mark 6, and generously grease the baking tin with olive oil.

Sift the flour and baking powder into a large mixing bowl, then add the polenta (or cornmeal), sugar and salt and mix in. Pour in the soured milk, add the creamed corn and the olive oil and stir together until combined.

Pour the cornbread batter into the prepared baking tin, sprinkle over the chilli flakes (if using) and a little extra sea salt and place in the oven to bake for 25–30 minutes or until firm to a light touch and slightly cracked on top. Leave the cornbread in its tin for 5 minutes before turning out and cutting into triangles (if serving warm) or leaving it to cool on a wire rack (if serving at room temperature).

sausage, lentil &
sun-dried tomato cassoulet

This recipe offers a twist on traditional cassoulet by combining sausages with lentils instead of haricot beans, and adding cubes of sweet potato. It has all the heartiness of the original, pepped up with a little mustard and some sun-dried tomatoes, which add a burst of intensity that goes so well with the earthy bite of the lentils. Serve with lightly steamed greens and, if you're in need of serious sustenance, a bowl of mashed potato.

nut free   gluten free   dairy free   egg free   soya free   yeast free

Serves 4

1 sweet potato
1 white onion
2 cloves of garlic
3 tbsp olive oil
Leaves from 3 sprigs
    of thyme
250g Puy lentils
1 litre chicken or vegetable
    stock (see the Glossary,
    page 232)
2 tsp English mustard
    (2 heaped tsp mustard
    powder mixed with 2 tsp
    water) or homemade
    mustard (see the Glossary,
    page 229)
100g sun-dried tomatoes
8 gluten-free sausages
A small bunch of flat-leaf
    parsley
Sea salt flakes and freshly
    ground black pepper

Peel the sweet potato, discarding the two ends, and chop into 1cm cubes. Roughly chop the onion and crush the garlic. Pour 2 tablespoons of the olive oil into a heavy-based casserole dish or saucepan and when the oil is hot, add the onion, garlic and thyme leaves. Season well with salt and pepper and fry over a low–medium heat for about 15 minutes or until the onion has softened but not browned.

Add the lentils and the sweet potato cubes to the casserole dish or saucepan, pour over the stock and bring to the boil. Reduce the heat to low and leave to simmer, partially covered with a lid, for 35–45 minutes or until the lentils are tender with just a little bite and the liquid has reduced to a depth of about 1cm. Stir in the mustard and sun-dried tomatoes, then remove from the heat and set aside.

Heat the remaining olive oil in a large frying pan, add the sausages and fry, turning regularly, over a medium–high heat for about 10 minutes or until browned all over. Transfer the sausages to the casserole dish or saucepan, pushing them down into the lentil mixture, then bring to a simmer, cover with the lid and leave to cook for a further 10–15 minutes or until the sausages are cooked through. Finely chop the parsley and scatter over the top before serving.

masala
chicken

Here, chicken is marinated in spices and coconut milk or almond cream to create a rich and aromatic sauce when the dish is cooked. By baking it in the oven, you end up with intensely flavoured, tender chicken with a peppery, crisp top. It's a delicious and simple way to make a fragrant curry – one that I like to serve with basmati rice and a coriander, tomato and onion salad to add a little bite. It also goes delightfully well with my Sweet Potato and Onion Bhajis (see page 162); add a few poppadoms and a little dhal (see page 160) and you have a veritable feast. I recommend you marinate the chicken in a large freezer bag; this helps the marinade to really penetrate the meat and enables you to turn the chicken pieces easily in the mixture without any mess or fuss.

nut free   gluten free   dairy free   egg free   soya free   yeast free

Serves 4

8 chicken thighs on the bone (skin left on)
Juice of 1 lemon
A small bunch of coriander
Sea salt flakes and freshly ground black pepper

For the marinade
250ml full-fat coconut milk
2.5cm piece of root ginger
4 cloves of garlic
1 tbsp tomato purée
½ tsp turmeric
1 heaped tsp chilli powder (or to taste)
1 tsp ground cumin
1 tsp ground coriander
1 tsp garam masala

Begin by scoring three cuts, about 1cm deep and evenly spaced, across each chicken thigh and then place in a sealable freezer bag. Pour the lemon juice over the chicken, season well with salt and pepper and set aside to tenderise for 20 minutes.

Meanwhile, prepare the marinade. Pour the coconut milk into a mixing bowl, finely grate the ginger and garlic into the bowl and stir in. Add the remaining ingredients for the marinade and stir together before pouring over the chicken thighs. Squeeze out any excess air from the bag, then seal and leave to marinate for a minimum of 1 hour or up to 24 hours. If marinating for longer than an hour, store in the fridge, then remove and bring up to room temperature before cooking.

When you are ready to cook the chicken, preheat the oven to 220°C (425°F), gas mark 7.

Tip the chicken thighs and marinade into a large, shallow casserole or ovenproof dish, making sure that the chicken is skin-side up. Cook, uncovered, in the oven for 40–45 minutes or until the chicken is tender and cooked through and the skin crisp on top. Finely chop the coriander and sprinkle over the chicken before serving.

dhal with
caraway aubergine

Rich, thick and creamy, this mellow dhal provides a delicious accompaniment to curries (my Masala Chicken or Creamy Chicken Curry both spring to mind – see pages 159 and 141). Served with my Sweet Potato and Onion Bhaji Bites (see page 162), it would also make a wonderful vegetarian option, with a bowl of basmati rice, a few poppadoms and some freshly sliced tomatoes to complete the spread. The caraway-roasted aubergine included in this recipe adds extra bite and a fragrant finish. I like my dhal quite thick, but you can always add a little extra water at the end of cooking if you prefer it to be a little thinner.

nut free   gluten free   vegan   soya free   yeast free

Serves 4

1 large aubergine
4 tbsp olive oil
1 tsp caraway seeds
½ tsp sea salt flakes
A small bunch of coriander

For the dahl
1 onion
1 clove of garlic
1cm piece of root ginger
1 tbsp olive oil
½ stick of cinnamon
½ tsp ground cumin
½ tsp turmeric
1 bay leaf
170g red lentils
600ml vegetable stock (see
    the Glossary, page 232)
½ tsp sea salt flakes
Juice of ½ lemon

Trim the ends from the aubergine and cut the flesh into 1cm chunks. Pour the olive oil into a mixing bowl and add the caraway seeds and sea salt. Mix together, then add the aubergine and toss in the oil. Set aside to marinate while you prepare the dhal.

Roughly chop the onion and finely grate the garlic and ginger. Heat the olive oil in a large saucepan, add the onion, garlic and ginger and fry over a low heat for about 20 minutes or until the onion has begun to soften. Add the spices and bay leaf to the pan and continue to fry for a further 3 minutes, then add the lentils and stir in until well coated in the spice mixture.

Pour over the stock, cover with a lid and bring to the boil, then reduce the heat and leave to simmer gently for 20 minutes (try not to stir the mixture as it cooks) or until nearly all of the liquid has been absorbed.

While the lentils are cooking, preheat the oven to 180°C (350°F), gas mark 4.

Tip the marinated aubergine onto a baking tray and roast in the oven for 30–35 minutes or until golden.

Take the lentils off the heat and beat vigorously with a wooden spoon into a smooth and creamy dhal. Stir in the salt and lemon juice, then spoon into a serving dish. Roughly chop the coriander and scatter over the hot dhal along with the roasted aubergine before serving.

sweet potato &
onion bhaji bites

These delicious oven-baked bhajis have all the flavour of their fried counterparts but are much creamier and lighter in texture. Baking them in the oven gives them a soft interior with a slightly crisp outer crust. They would be perfect as a starter, served with a green salad and some freshly sliced ripe mango, or as part of a curry feast with a large bowl of basmati rice and my baked Masala Chicken and Dhal with Caraway Aubergine (see pages 159 and 160). Or, indeed, you could have them as part of a picnic or packed lunch, their size making them nicely transportable. You can easily make them in advance, warming them up in a hot oven for 5–10 minutes before serving at the table.

nut free   gluten free   vegan   soya free   yeast free

Makes about 15 bhajis

1 large sweet potato
1 x 400g tin of chickpeas, drained and rinsed
2 red onions
2 tbsp olive oil, plus extra for greasing
1cm piece of root ginger
2 cloves of garlic
1 fresh red chilli
1 tsp curry powder
1 tsp ground cumin
1 tsp turmeric
A small bunch of coriander
4 tbsp gram flour
1 tbsp lemon juice
Sea salt flakes and freshly ground black pepper

Peel and cut the sweet potato into 2.5cm chunks, then place in a steamer or colander set over a saucepan and add the chickpeas. Steam over 3cm of simmering water for 15 minutes or until the sweet potato is soft and collapsing.

Meanwhile, halve the onions and slice into thin half-moons. Heat 1 tablespoon of the olive oil in a frying pan, add the onions and fry over a low–medium heat for 15 minutes or until softened but not browned.

While the onions are cooking, finely grate the ginger, crush the garlic and deseed and finely chop the chilli. Add these to the onions, along with the spices, and fry for a further 2–3 minutes.

Preheat the oven to 200°C (400°F), gas mark 6, and grease a large baking tray with olive oil.

Finely chop the coriander, then transfer the steamed sweet potato and chickpeas to a food processor and blitz until you have a coarse purée. Turn out into a mixing bowl and add the softened spiced onions, gram flour, lemon juice, chopped coriander and remaining olive oil. Season with salt and pepper and stir together until combined.

Scoop out heaped tablespoons of the mixture and shape into little round patties about 2.5cm in diameter. (You may want to wash your hands straight after shaping the patties as the turmeric can stain your fingers yellow!) Place the bhajis on the greased baking tray and bake in the oven for 40 minutes – carefully turning them over after 20 minutes – or until they are crisp and golden. Serve warm from the oven or leave to cool.

baby squash with
leeks & garlic & herb cheese

This is yet another way to use my versatile Garlic and Herb Cashew Cream Cheese (see page 56). Here, it is mixed with softened leeks and used to stuff baby squash. It's the loveliest way to serve squash on an autumnal evening: a little freshly baked Cornbread (see page 156) and a large salad are the only accompaniments needed. If you fancy ringing the changes a little, then a handful of roughly chopped chestnuts, crispy fried smoked bacon lardons or a scattering of toasted pine nuts would all make a welcome addition.

contains nuts   gluten free   vegan   soya free   yeast free

Serves 6

6 individual baby squash
   (acorn or pumpkin)
6 leeks
2 tbsp olive oil
1 portion of Garlic and Herb
   Cashew Cream Cheese
   (see page 56)
Sea salt flakes and freshly
   ground black pepper

Preheat the oven to 190°C (375°F), gas mark 5.

Slice the tops from the baby squash, setting them aside to use as 'lids', and carefully scoop out any seeds and pith, being sure not to break the skin at any point. Place the squash in a large roasting tin, slicing a little off the base from each one if necessary to help them stand upright.

Trim the leeks, discarding any tough green leaves, and finely chop. Heat the olive oil in a large saucepan or frying pan and then gently fry the leeks over a low–medium heat for about 20 minutes or until softened but not browned. Remove from the heat and stir into the Garlic and Herb Cashew Cream Cheese, seasoning with salt and pepper to taste.

Spoon the leek filling into the baby squash and carefully place their lids back on top. Bake in the oven for 1–1½ hours or until cooked through and tender to the point of a knife and then serve.

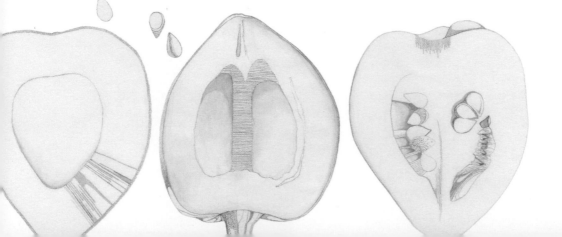

chicken &
preserved lemon tagine

Preserved lemons are a common ingredient in Middle Eastern cooking. A softer and plumper version of their fresh counterparts, they are slightly less sour but somehow much more powerful-tasting. A little goes a long way, but they make an amazing addition to salads, roasted vegetables and, in this case, tagines. Mixed with the other ingredients in here, the flavours are light, slightly piquant and zesty, the chicken rich and tender. The dish would go really well with my velvety Butter Bean Hummus with Mint Oil and served with a huge bowl of Quinoa Tabbouleh (see pages 173 and 66). Make the tagine a day ahead, if you can; not only will it free you up the following day, but also the flavours will really have time to develop.

nut free   *gluten free*   *dairy free*   *egg free*   *soya free*   *yeast free*

Serves 4–6

4 chicken breasts
    (skin left on)
1 large onion
3 cloves of garlic
1 red pepper
3 tbsp olive oil
2 tsp cumin seeds
2 tsp ground coriander
5cm stick of cinnamon
1 x 400g tin of chopped
    tomatoes
570ml chicken or vegetable
    stock (see the Glossary,
    page 232)
4 preserved lemons (see
    the Glossary, page 231)
100g soft dried apricots
1 small bunch of flat-leaf
    parsley
Sea salt flakes and freshly
    ground black pepper

Equipment
You will need a flameproof
    tagine or heavy-based
    casserole dish with a lid
    for this recipe

Preheat the oven to 150°C (300°F), gas mark 2.

Begin by slicing each chicken breast diagonally into 3–4 pieces, depending on its size. Roughly chop the onion, crush the garlic and slice the pepper into 2cm-thick strips, discarding the seeds and stalk.

Heat 2 tablespoons of the olive oil in the tagine or casserole dish, season the skin of the chicken with salt and pepper and place in the hot oil, skin-side down. Fry over a medium heat for 3–4 minutes on each side or until the skin is golden and the meat sealed. You may have to do this in two batches, depending on the size of your tagine or casserole dish – overloading the pot will stop the chicken from browning.

Remove the chicken from the tagine or casserole dish and set aside. Pour the remaining oil into the tagine, add the onion and red pepper and fry over a low–medium heat for about 10 minutes or until starting to soften. Add the garlic, cumin seeds, coriander and cinnamon to the tagine and fry for a further 2 minutes.

Return the chicken to the tagine and pour over the chopped tomatoes and stock. Cut the preserved lemons in half and then add them, along with the apricots, to the tagine. Bring to a rolling simmer and then cover with the lid and cook in the oven for 1½–2 hours or until the chicken is cooked through and tender and the sauce is rich.

Finely chop the fresh parsley. Remove the tagine from the oven, stir in the herbs and serve.

creamy
caponata bake

This creamy, comforting dish has all the flavour of a traditional caponata (a cooked vegetable salad with added capers, olives and raisins), but with the varied textures of a lasagne. Here, layers of aubergine stand in for the 'pasta' sheets, adding body and a meaty counterpart to the creamy sauce. It's a very satisfying and hearty combination, and delicious when served with a leafy green salad and some freshly baked Focaccia (see page 180).

contains nuts   gluten free   vegan   soya free   yeast free

Serves 6

2 large aubergines
2 tbsp olive oil
A handful of pine nuts,
    for sprinkling

For the caponata
500g courgettes
1 large white onion
2 ripe tomatoes
2 tbsp olive oil
1 head of celery
1 heaped tbsp raisins
1 tbsp tomato purée
20 pitted green olives
1 heaped tbsp capers,
    drained and rinsed
1 tbsp soft light brown sugar
Juice of ½ lemon

For the cream sauce
300g cashew nuts
100g pine nuts
Juice of ½ lemon
½ tsp sea salt flakes
1 tbsp olive oil

Equipment
You will need a 22cm x 30cm
    rectangular baking dish,
    about 7cm deep, for
    this recipe

Begin by soaking the cashew nuts and pine nuts for the cream sauce in water for 3–6 hours.

Next, make the caponata. Trim the courgettes, then cut these and the onion and tomatoes into 1–2cm chunks. Heat the olive oil in a large saucepan and fry the onion over a low–medium heat for about 5 minutes or until starting to soften. Add the courgettes and continue to fry for around 10 minutes or until tender and starting to soften at the edges but not brown.

Trim the ends from the celery and slice into fine rounds. Add the celery to the saucepan with the tomatoes, raisins, tomato purée, olives, capers, sugar and lemon juice. Stir all the ingredients together and leave to cook, uncovered, over a low heat for about 30 minutes or until all the vegetables have softened.

While the caponata is cooking, drain the nuts and place in a high-powered blender with the lemon juice, salt, olive oil and 120ml of water. Blitz until completely smooth and creamy, scraping down the sides of the blender jug every now and then. You want the mixture to be very smooth and velvety, so keep blitzing until it reaches the desired consistency.

Preheat the oven to 180°C (350°F), gas mark 4.

Next, trim the ends from the aubergines and slice lengthways into 3–4mm-thick strips. Cover the aubergine slices in cold water and leave for 5 minutes – this will stop them absorbing too much oil when you fry them. Drain in a colander and then toss in the olive oil. Heat a large frying pan or griddle pan until hot and fry the aubergine slices, a few at a time, over a medium–high heat for 1–2 minutes on each side or until lightly charred and softened.

Spread half of the caponata evenly over the base of the baking dish. Cover with half the aubergine slices, in an even layer, and then smooth over half of the creamy nut mixture. Repeat with a final layer of caponata, then aubergine and the remaining creamy nut mixture. Scatter over a handful of pine nuts and then bake in the oven for 30 minutes or until bubbling and the pine nuts are golden.

If you want a slightly heartier version of this dish then you can replace the aubergines with a large bowlful of cooked rice. Simply layer the caponata in the base of the dish, cover with a layer of cooked rice and then layer over the creamy nut mixture and bake as usual...

chestnut
& chorizo stew

nut-free option

This is a wonderfully warming kind of dish, perfect for cold wintry nights. The combination of piquant chorizo and earthy–sweet chestnuts works particularly well, though if you wanted to make this recipe nut free you could replace the chestnuts with chickpeas or butter beans. Serve with a bowl of rice or mashed potato; it would also taste delicious with some of my freshly baked Roasted Vegetable Socca or Sweet Potato Bread (see pages 71 and 78) to mop up all the juices. Make sure you check the chorizo for any milk proteins or wheat – some varieties do contain them (see the Glossary, page 226, for recommended suppliers).

contains nuts   *nut-free option*   *gluten free*   *dairy free*   *egg free*   *soya free*   *yeast free*

Serves 2 generously

1 large onion
2 cloves of garlic
200g chorizo
1 tbsp olive oil
½ tsp ground cinnamon
1 tsp cumin seeds
2 tbsp tomato purée
240g tinned chestnuts (or tinned chickpeas or butter beans for a nut-free option)
1 x 400g tin of chopped tomatoes
A small bunch of flat-leaf parsley

Finely chop the onion and crush the garlic. Slice the chorizo into 1cm half-moons and set aside.

Heat the oil in a heavy-based casserole dish, then add the chorizo and fry over a medium–high heat for 5 minutes or until starting to crisp and release its piquant oils. Scoop out with a slotted spoon and set aside. Add the onion and garlic to the dish, reduce the heat and fry very gently for about 20 minutes or until soft and slightly caramelised.

Add the spices and tomato purée to the dish and fry for a further 5 minutes – this will cook the tomato purée and add a richer flavour to the stew. Add the chestnuts (or chickpeas or butter beans) and chorizo, pour over the chopped tomatoes and then fill the empty tin half full with water and add that to the dish, too. Bring to the boil, then reduce the heat and leave to simmer gently, covered with a lid, for 10 minutes.

Finely chop the parsley and scatter over the stew before serving.

fireside suppers

nut-free
option

lamb, apricot & tahini meatballs

These meatballs are made with a lovely mixture of minced lamb, finely diced onion and apricots, bound together with a little tahini and cooked in a delicately spiced and fragrant sauce. And you can dress them up or down, depending on the occasion; serve them as they are with a helping of basmati rice for a quick and easy supper, or scatter over sliced black olives and chopped parsley and serve with Quinoa Tabbouleh and Butter Bean Hummus (see pages 66 and 173) for a more elaborate spread.

contains nuts   *nut-free option*   *gluten free*   *dairy free*   *egg free*   *soya free*   *yeast free*

Serves 4 (makes 18 meatballs)

1 onion
2 tbsp olive oil
50g soft dried apricots
500g lean minced lamb
1 tbsp tahini (or sunflower
    seed butter for a nut-free
    option – see the Glossary,
    pages 232–3)
2 cloves of garlic
1½ x 400g tins of chopped
    tomatoes
1 tbsp lemon juice
1 tsp soft light brown sugar
Sea salt flakes and freshly
    ground black pepper

For the spice mixture
1 tsp cumin seeds
1 tsp coriander seeds
½ tsp black mustard seeds
½ tsp ground cinnamon
½ tsp chilli flakes
1 tsp dried mint
¼ tsp sea salt flakes

First, finely chop the onion. Heat half the olive oil in a frying pan and gently fry the onion over a low–medium heat for about 10 minutes or until soft but not browned. Remove from the heat and allow to cool down.

Finely chop the apricots and place in a large mixing bowl with the mince, tahini (or sunflower seed butter) and cooked onion. Season generously with salt and pepper and mix and mash all the ingredients together with a fork until combined. Using your hands, shape the mixture into balls approximately 2.5cm in diameter.

Next, prepare the spice mixture. Place the cumin, coriander and mustard seeds in a small heavy-based frying pan and dry-fry over a medium heat for 2–3 minutes or until lightly toasted and fragrant. Remove from the heat, place in a mortar, then add the cinnamon, chilli flakes, mint and salt, and grind with a pestle into a fine powder. Alternatively, place in a freezer bag and crush with a rolling pin.

Heat the remaining oil in a large heavy-based pan and fry the meatballs over a low–medium heat, shaking the pan regularly, for 5–8 minutes or until browned all over. (Depending on the size of your pan, you may have to do this in two batches, as trying to fit too many meatballs in at a time will mean they won't brown properly.) Use a slotted spoon to scoop out the meatballs and set aside.

Next, crush the garlic and add to the pan with the ground spices, frying gently for a minute or two. Pour over the chopped tomatoes, add the lemon juice and sugar, then return the meatballs to the pan. Leave to simmer for a further 8–10 minutes before seasoning the sauce with salt and pepper to taste and serving.

chickpea pancakes

These pancakes are inspired by besan cheela, traditional Indian savoury pancakes, much like chapatti, made from gram (chickpea) flour and served as an accompaniment to curries and chutneys. My version, made denser by the inclusion of coarsely chopped chickpeas, is intended as a kind of bread or wrap. Fill with hummus and a little Carrot and Orange Salad (see page 68), then roll up to enclose the filling and you have a perfect lunch. Or serve alongside Moroccan Vegetable Tagine (see page 142), using the pancakes to scoop up the fragrant sauce, or use to accompany my Creamy Chicken Curry, Dhal with Caraway Aubergine or Masala Chicken (see pages 141, 160 and 159). You could add a bit of spice, too: a little ground coriander and cumin or a pinch of chilli flakes and caraway seeds would all work beautifully. Once made, these pancakes will keep for a day or two wrapped in cling film in the fridge; you can also reheat them in the oven or in a frying pan (dry-frying them for a minute or so on each side).

nut free *gluten free* *vegan* *soya free* *yeast free*

Makes 6 pancakes

1 x 400g tin of chickpeas, drained and rinsed
150g gram flour
250ml rice milk
1 tbsp olive oil, plus extra for frying
A good pinch of sea salt flakes

Equipment
You will need an 18–20cm non-stick frying pan for this recipe

Place the chickpeas in a food processor and roughly blitz to a coarse breadcrumb texture. Alternatively, finely chop by hand.

Combine the gram flour, rice milk and olive oil in a large mixing bowl and whisk together vigorously. Alternatively, you can whizz them together in a food processor. Add the chickpeas and salt and fold into the pancake batter.

Heat a little oil (about 1 teaspoon) in the frying pan – a non-stick one is essential here. Add a ladleful of batter (that's about 5 tablespoons or 80ml) and use a spatula to help swirl it round the pan to form a pancake about 13cm in diameter. Cook over a gentle heat until the pancake is almost dry on the top and golden on the bottom. Flip the pancake over and cook until the other side is golden, too – about 3 minutes on each side.

Continue until you have used all of the batter, adding a little extra oil to the pan between pancakes if necessary and keeping the cooked pancakes wrapped in foil in a warm oven.

contains
nuts

butter bean
hummus with mint oil

For those suffering from food intolerances, hummus can be an absolute life-saver. Quick to make, packed full of protein and with a rich and creamy texture that one so often craves, it is great to have on hand, and so versatile, too. You can spread it on toast, serve it as a dip with crudités, as a filling for baked potatoes or a sauce for salads or roasted vegetables. This butter bean version is oh-so-simple and produces the most wonderfully creamy texture, but without all the long overnight cooking of dried chickpeas involved in the conventional version of the dish. The flavour is just divine, too, the mint oil adding a touch of sweetness, colour and texture. Serve it alongside Lemon and Oregano Lamb Kebabs, Quinoa Tabbouleh, Chicken and Preserved Lemon Tagine and, of course, my Moroccan Vegetable Tagine and Lamb, Apricot and Tahini Meatballs (see pages 64, 66, 165, 142 and 171).

contains nuts   *gluten free*   *vegan*   *soya free*   *yeast free*

Serves 4–6

1 x 400g tin of butter beans,
    drained and rinsed
1 tbsp tahini
Juice of 1 small lemon
3–4 tbsp extra-virgin olive oil
½ tsp sea salt flakes
Freshly ground black pepper

For the mint oil
Leaves from a small bunch
    of mint
2 tbsp extra-virgin olive oil

Place all of the ingredients (except those for the mint oil) in a food processor, along with 2 tablespoons of water, and blitz until completely smooth, adding more water or oil if you think it needs it and seasoning with pepper and extra salt to taste.

Place the mint leaves in a mortar, pour over a little of the olive oil and grind with a pestle until the leaves are broken down and have infused the oil with their scent. Stir in the remaining olive oil and drizzle the mint oil over the hummus.

pea soup with
crispy chorizo croutons
butternut squash, lentil, honey
& thyme soup
baked leg of lamb
with lemon, garlic & oregano
focaccia
grilled tiger prawns
with avocado cream
patatas bravas
bread & melon soup
poached chicken
with walnut sauce
chicken with caraway,
olives & orange
sweet & sour chicken
lemon & ginger chicken
stir-fry jasmine rice
lamb burgers
with beetroot hummus
spicy bean burgers
with avocado salsa
herb-crusted rack of lamb with
sloe gin gravy & butter bean mash

weekend feasts

pea soup with
crispy chorizo croutons

Frozen peas are the most versatile of convenience foods. Cooked in a trice, they can be added to salads, risotto, pasta or, as here, made into a gloriously fresh, vibrant soup. You could use fresh peas instead, of course, especially some straight from the garden. The fennel adds a lovely aniseed note, while the split peas give the soup body and a little extra soul. You could serve it just like this, with perhaps some freshly baked Focaccia (see page 180) on the side, for a vegetarian meal. But the crispy chorizo adds a salty bite that perfectly counterbalances the natural sweetness of the peas. Be sure to check it for any allergens, however. Like most things, the better the quality, the purer the ingredients (see the Glossary, page 226, for recommended suppliers).

nut free   *gluten free*   *dairy free*   *egg free*   *soya free*   *yeast free*

Serves 4

1 fennel bulb
1 white onion
1 tbsp olive oil
100g yellow split peas
300g frozen peas
1.2 litres vegetable stock (see the Glossary, page 232)
200g chorizo
Sea salt flakes and freshly ground black pepper

Trim the fennel and roughly chop this and the onion. Heat the olive oil in a large saucepan and fry the onion and fennel over a low–medium heat for 10–15 minutes or until softened but not browned.

Stir in the split peas and the frozen peas and then pour over the vegetable stock. Bring to a simmer and leave to cook gently, uncovered, for 20 minutes or until the split peas are tender. Once cooked, use a hand–held blender or food processor to blitz the mixture until smooth and creamy. Season with salt and pepper to taste.

Meanwhile, slice the chorizo into 5mm rounds. Heat a heavy-based frying pan and dry-fry the chorizo over a medium heat for 5–7 minutes or until starting to crisp and release its piquant oils.

Ladle the soup into bowls, then top with a handful of chorizo croutons and a drizzle of the spiced chorizo oil and serve.

butternut squash,
lentil, honey & thyme soup

Packed with nutrients and full of flavour, this soup is one of my absolute favourites. I love the earthy combination of butternut squash and lentils, the natural sweetness of the squash enhanced by the honey and the thyme lending an added aroma. Make it for a warming lunch, served with my Chickpea Bread (see page 28), or for a sustaining supper with Focaccia, fresh out of the oven, and perhaps my Chicory, Ham, Sweet Potato and Sun-dried Tomato Salad (see pages 180 and 88).

nut free   gluten free   vegan   soya free   yeast free

Serves 4

1 butternut squash
2½ tbsp olive oil
Leaves from a small bunch of thyme
1 small onion
4 sticks of celery
100g red lentils
1.2 litres vegetable or chicken stock (see the Glossary, page 232)
1 rounded tsp runny honey
Sea salt flakes and freshly ground black pepper

Preheat the oven to 200°C (400°F), gas mark 6.

Peel and halve the butternut squash and scoop out the pith and seeds with a spoon. Chop the flesh into 1cm chunks and place in a large roasting tin. Add 1½ tablespoons of the olive oil and the thyme leaves and mix in with the squash. Season well with salt and pepper and roast in the oven for 35 minutes or until the squash is beginning to turn golden at the edges.

Meanwhile, finely chop the onion and celery. Heat the remaining olive oil in a large saucepan and fry the onion and celery over a low–medium heat for 10–15 minutes or until completely softened but not browned.

Add the lentils, stirring these into the pan, and pour over the stock. Bring to the boil, then reduce the heat and leave to simmer gently for 10 minutes.

Once the squash is roasted, transfer to the mixture in the saucepan, add the honey and use a hand-held blender to blitz until smooth. Season with salt and pepper to taste and serve hot.

baked leg of lamb
with lemon, garlic & oregano

Here the traditional northern French dish of lamb cooked on top of boulangère potatoes (finely sliced with onions) is given a Greek twist with the addition of lemon, garlic and oregano. Preserved lemons are readily available from supermarkets and specialist shops, although you can easily make them yourself (see the Glossary, page 231). They are ideal for mingling with the roasted potatoes, imbuing them with an intense flavour that sits well with the rich meat and aromatic herbs and garlic.

nut free   *gluten free*   *dairy free*   *egg free*   *soya free*   *yeast free*

Serves 6

1.8kg floury potatoes
2 red onions
8 cloves of garlic
2 preserved lemons (see the Glossary, page 231)
A small bunch of oregano
3 tbsp olive oil
100ml chicken stock (see the Glossary, page 232)
1 x 2.4kg leg of lamb
1 heaped tsp dried oregano
Sea salt flakes and freshly ground black pepper

Preheat the oven to 200°C (400°F), gas mark 6.

Begin by slicing the potatoes (no need to peel them) into 2–3mm-thick rounds. Halve the onions and slice into half-moons 3mm thick, then peel the garlic cloves. Cut the preserved lemons into rounds approximately the same thickness as the onions.

Spread half of the sliced potatoes and onions evenly over the base of a roasting tin and scatter over half of the oregano sprigs and sliced lemons and four of the garlic cloves. Season well with salt and pepper and then spread the remaining potatoes and onions evenly over the top, scattering over the last slices of lemon. Season well again, pour over 2 tablespoons of the olive oil and all of the stock.

Slice each of the remaining garlic cloves lengthways into three slivers. Using a small sharp knife, make incisions, each approximately 2cm deep, all over the lamb. Insert a garlic shard wrapped in an oregano sprig into each of the incisions, pushing the garlic in as much as possible.

Place the lamb on top of the potatoes. Drizzle the remaining oil over the lamb, season well with salt and pepper and scatter with the dried oregano. For a medium-cooked joint, bake in the oven for 1½ hours, or approximately 18 minutes for every 500g of lamb.

Remove from the oven, cover the tin with foil and set aside to rest for 10 minutes before serving.

focaccia

Focaccia, with its slightly crisp, golden exterior and light, aerated interior, is a traditional Italian bread. Usually studded with fresh herbs and drizzled with best-quality extra-virgin olive oil, it should have an uneven texture inside, lightened by the olive oil that seeps through into the dough. I love this particular version, free from the yeast that so often dominates; I use baking powder instead to help leaven the bread a little. I've topped it with rosemary leaves here, but you could use any woody herb of your choice or a combination of olives, sun-dried tomatoes and herbs. An excellent lunchtime staple and even holding its own as a dinner-party accompaniment, this bread is delicious at any time of day.

nut free   gluten free   vegan   soya free   yeast free

Serves 6 as an accompaniment

225g gluten-free plain flour (ideally Doves Farm)
4 tsp gluten-free baking powder
¼ tsp xanthan gum
1 heaped tsp egg replacer (ideally Orgran) whisked with 2 tbsp water
1 tbsp olive oil, plus extra for greasing

For the topping
Leaves from 4 sprigs of rosemary
1–2 tbsp extra-virgin olive oil
Sea salt flakes

Equipment
You will need a 16cm x 24cm baking tin, about 4cm deep, for this recipe

Preheat the oven to 200°C (400°F), gas mark 6, and liberally grease the baking tin with olive oil.

Sift the flour, baking powder and xanthan gum into the bowl of a food processor and add the egg replacer mixture and olive oil. Pour over 250ml of hot water and blitz until you have a smooth and creamy dough – it should be dropping consistency rather than completely liquid. Alternatively, place the egg replacer mixture in a large mixing bowl (or make the mixture in the bowl), add the remaining dry ingredients, stir together and then gradually add the oil and water, beating together until smooth and creamy.

Pour the mixture into the prepared tin, then level the top with the back of a spoon, pushing it into the corners of the tin and spreading it evenly. Using a fingertip, make little dents all over the dough. (Because it is such a liquid batter, you won't be able to make solid holes, just little peaks and troughs in the surface of the bread.)

Next, scatter over the rosemary leaves, drizzle over the olive oil and sprinkle a few sea salt flakes on top of the dough. Bake in the oven for 35 minutes or until just golden and crisp on top. Remove from the oven, turn out onto a wire rack and leave to cool for a few minutes. Serve while warm or leave to cool completely before slicing.

grilled tiger prawns
with avocado cream

This is such a simple summery supper dish, perfect for serving with Patatas Bravas (see page 184) and a large green salad. The prawns are lightly seasoned with smoked paprika to bring out their natural sweetness, which is complemented in turn by the avocado cream with its rich, fresh flavour. This would be perfect for serving as a starter or as a nibble – just make sure there's a bowl of lemon water about, as you're sure to get your hands mucky!

nut free   *gluten free*   *dairy free*   *egg free*   *soya free*   *yeast free*

Serves 4 as a starter or accompaniment

16 large raw tiger prawns (peeled and deveined and ideally with the shell still attached to the tails)
2 tbsp olive oil
½ tsp smoked paprika
1 tbsp lemon juice
½ tsp soft light brown sugar
Sea salt flakes and freshly ground black pepper

For the avocado cream
2 ripe avocados (preferably Hass)
1 tbsp garlic oil or extra-virgin olive oil
1 tbsp lemon juice

Equipment
You will need 4 metal or bamboo skewers for this recipe

Begin by soaking the bamboo skewers (if using) in water for half an hour; this is to prevent them from burning under the grill. Place the prawns in a bowl with the olive oil, paprika, lemon juice and sugar, then season with salt and pepper and leave to marinate for 30 minutes.

When the prawns have finished marinating, preheat the grill to high. Thread the prawns onto the skewers and grill for 1–2 minutes or until just turning pink and starting to curl slightly. Turn the skewers over and grill for a further 1–2 minutes or until just cooked through.

While the prawns are cooking, make the avocado cream. Halve the avocados, scoop out the ripe flesh (discarding the stones) and place in a food processer with the oil and lemon juice. Season with a little salt and pepper and blitz until smooth and glossy. Taste and add a little extra lemon juice or seasoning if you think it needs it.

Serve the prawns immediately with the avocado cream on the side to dip into.

patatas bravas

This classic Spanish tapas dish really lends itself to allergen-free eating; it's also exceptionally delicious and ideal as part of a larger spread. I always serve it with my Grilled Tiger Prawns with Avocado Cream (see page 182) and a large green salad scattered with olives and drizzled with lemon juice and olive oil. It also goes beautifully with seared chorizo sausage and a green bean and almond salad. I like to push the finished sauce through a sieve so that it's nice and smooth, but if you don't have time or the inclination, it tastes just as good if you miss that step out.

nut free   *gluten free*   *vegan*   *soya free*   *yeast free*

Serves 4 as an accompaniment

1kg waxy potatoes (or new potatoes if they're in season)
2 tbsp olive oil
½ tsp sea salt flakes

For the tomato sauce
1 onion
2 cloves of garlic
2 tbsp olive oil
1 tbsp tomato purée
1 tsp smoked paprika
½ tsp chilli flakes
1 x 400g tin of chopped tomatoes
A small bunch of flat-leaf parsley
Sea salt flakes and freshly ground black pepper

Begin by making the sauce. Finely chop the onion and crush the garlic. Heat the olive oil in a saucepan, add the onion and a pinch of salt and fry over a low–medium heat for about 10 minutes or until softened but not browned.

Add the garlic, tomato purée, smoked paprika and chilli to the pan and fry for a further 5 minutes, stirring every now and then. Pour over the chopped tomatoes, bring to a simmer and then leave to cook gently for 10 minutes or until the sauce is thickened and slightly reduced. Season with salt and pepper to taste and set aside.

Meanwhile, preheat the oven to 200°C (400°F), gas mark 6.

Cut the potatoes (no need to peel them) into 2–3cm dice. Pour the olive oil into a large roasting tin, throw in the potatoes, then scatter over the salt and mix together so that the potatoes are well coated in the oil. Roast in the oven for 45–50 minutes or until crisp and golden.

Meanwhile, pass the finished sauce through a fine-mesh sieve until smooth. Return the sauce to a clean pan and heat through, then finely chop the parsley. Serve the potatoes piled high, with the sauce poured over and the parsley scattered on top.

contains nuts

tomato
& almond soup

This particular dish is my take on a cream of tomato soup and would be perfect at any time of year. The simple, clean flavours of tomatoes and onions are enriched with ground almonds, which serve to both thicken and add creaminess to the soup. The finished soup is topped with a medley of sun-dried tomatoes, toasted almonds and coriander, adding a pleasing burst of flavour and crunch that's essential to the dish.

contains nuts   *gluten free*   *vegan*   *soya free*   *yeast free*

Serves 4

A handful of flaked almonds
2 cloves of garlic
A small bunch of coriander
200g ripe tomatoes
4 sun-dried tomatoes
2 tbsp extra-virgin olive oil, plus extra for drizzling
1 x 400g tin of chopped tomatoes
½ tsp soft light brown sugar
350ml vegetable stock (see the Glossary, page 232)
6 tbsp ground almonds
Sea salt flakes and freshly ground black pepper

In a small heavy-based saucepan, dry-fry the almonds over a medium–high heat, shaking the pan regularly to stop them catching, for 4–5 minutes or until lightly toasted. Remove from the heat and set aside while you prepare the soup.

Crush the garlic and finely chop the coriander. Roughly chop the fresh tomatoes and finely slice the sun-dried tomatoes into strips. Pour the olive oil into a large saucepan and add the tinned and fresh tomatoes with the garlic. Bring to the boil, then reduce the heat and leave to simmer for 10 minutes. Add the sugar and stock, season well with salt and pepper and simmer for a further 20 minutes.

Stir in the ground almonds and, using a food processor or hand-held blender, blitz the mixture until smooth. Ladle the soup into individual bowls, scatter over the sun-dried tomatoes, toasted almonds and coriander, then lightly drizzle with olive oil to serve.

poached chicken
with walnut sauce

An interpretation of a classic Turkish dish, this is a jewel of a recipe. The flavours are light but with a smoky quality from the extravagant quantities of paprika and toasted walnuts. You can make this whole dish ahead of time and then store it in the fridge for a few hours, but be sure to take it out a good half an hour before serving, as the sauce is best when served at room temperature. Use your favourite intolerance-friendly bread for this recipe, or indeed any of the breads in this book (see Chickpea Bread, Sweet Potato Bread and Cornbread on pages 28, 78 and 156). Alternatively, you could use cooked quinoa or rice instead of bread, although it won't have quite the same effect.

contains nuts   *gluten free*   *dairy free*   *egg free*   *soya free*   *yeast free*

Serves 4

A small bunch of coriander
Juice of 1 lemon
4 skinless chicken breasts
    (at room temperature)
225g shelled walnuts
1 large clove of garlic
2 slices of allergen-free
    bread of your choice
1 tbsp walnut oil
2 tbsp smoked paprika
12 pitted black olives
Sea salt flakes

Trim the stalks from the coriander (keeping the leaves aside for later) and place in a large saucepan filled with water. Add a big pinch of salt and the lemon juice, then cover with a lid and bring to the boil. When the water is boiling, add the chicken breasts, cover again with the lid and remove from the heat. Leave the pan to sit for 50–60 minutes before draining the chicken breasts, reserving half of the stock to use later. (Cooking the chicken like this allows it to poach slowly, retaining the tenderness of the meat and adding a delicate flavour from the lemon and coriander.) Leave the chicken to rest for 20 minutes before slicing.

Preheat the oven to 180°C (350°F), gas mark 4, and scatter the walnuts on a baking tray. Roast in the oven, shaking the tray occasionally to stop them burning, for about 8 minutes or until lightly toasted and fragrant. Remove from the oven and set aside to cool down.

Place the toasted walnuts in a food processor, add a good pinch of salt and blitz into a coarse paste. Lightly crush the garlic and briefly soak the two slices of bread in the chicken stock – about 30 seconds should do it. Carefully squeeze the bread out and add to the walnuts, along with the garlic. Blitz again until you have a thick and smooth paste.

Keeping the food processor running, start adding the chicken-poaching stock, a little at a time and allowing the mixture to emulsify, until you have a thick and creamy sauce – you'll need about 250ml of liquid. Transfer to a bowl and set aside.

Pour the walnut oil into a small saucepan, add the paprika and heat gently for about 5 minutes or until the oil becomes a rich red colour. Remove from the heat and set aside to cool down; in that time the paprika will settle to the bottom of the pan.

Meanwhile, slice the chicken breasts diagonally into 1cm-thick slices. Lay the chicken on a large serving platter, overlapping in places. Pour the walnut sauce over the sliced meat and then drizzle over the red spiced oil, leaving the paprika in the bottom of the pan. Scatter over the reserved coriander leaves and the olives and then serve.

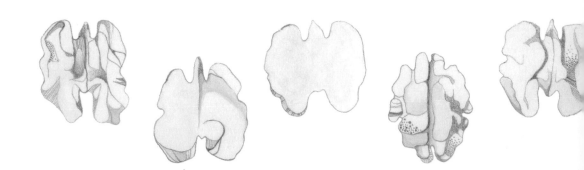

chicken with caraway, olives & orange

This dish is best served simply: warm from the oven with a green leaf salad and some freshly baked Sweet Potato Bread (see page 78) to mop up the juices, or with a bowl of basmati rice and an orange and mint salad. It's a divine combination of flavours: the moist tenderness of the chicken offset by the rich intensity of the oil-soaked onions and celery, the aromatic bite of the caraway and the sour–sweet tang of the orange and olives. Glorious to eat, it's also a breeze to put together, making it ideal for serving to family and friends for a relaxed weekend meal.

nut free   *gluten free*   *dairy free*   *egg free*   *soya free*   *yeast free*

Serves 4–6

4 onions
6 sticks of celery
3 cloves of garlic
50ml good-quality olive oil
1 x 1.75kg chicken (at room temperature)
Grated zest and juice of 1 orange
1 heaped tsp caraway seeds
A small bunch of coriander
20 pitted black olives
Sea salt flakes and freshly ground black pepper

Preheat the oven to 180°C (350°F), gas mark 4.

Halve and slice the onions into thin half-moons, trim the celery and cut into 4cm lengths, then finely slice the garlic into rounds. Place in a large casserole dish, pour over the olive oil and season well with salt and pepper before mixing together.

Place the chicken on top of the vegetables, pour over the orange juice and then scatter the caraway seeds and orange zest over the skin of the chicken. Season well with salt and pepper, cover with a lid and roast in the oven for 1½ hours, removing the lid for the last 15 minutes of cooking to allow the chicken to brown.

Once cooked, remove from the oven and set aside to rest for a minimum of 15 minutes. Lift out the chicken and carve into large pieces, keeping the thighs and legs whole and cutting the breasts into 2–3 sections.

Using a slotted spoon, scoop out the softened onions and celery and spread over a large serving platter. You can then either discard the remaining oil or pour it over the onions and celery, depending on your preference. Roughly chop the coriander, then lay the chicken pieces on top of the onions and scatter over the olives and coriander to serve.

sweet & sour chicken

This recipe has all the elements of a standard sweet and sour dish, including the lovely crisp crunch of the peppers, while keeping it healthy and, most importantly, allergen free. I think there is no better way to serve this than with a helping of basmati rice or Stir-fry Jasmine Rice (see page 191) and a generous portion of lightly steamed sugar snap peas. Scatter with roasted cashew nuts or drizzle with toasted sesame oil as the final touch, unless the dish needs to be entirely nut free.

nut free   gluten free   dairy free   egg free   soya free   yeast free

Serves 4

4 skinless chicken breasts
1 tbsp tamarind paste
½ tsp smoked paprika
½ tsp turmeric
A pinch of sea salt flakes
1 red pepper
1 yellow pepper
1 red onion
1 clove of garlic
2 spring onions
A bunch of fresh coriander
2 tbsp olive oil
Juice of ½ lime
150ml apple juice
1 tsp cornflour

Slice the chicken breasts into 3cm chunks and then place in a resealable freezer bag. Add the tamarind paste, paprika, turmeric and salt, squeeze out any excess air from the bag and seal. Massage the marinade into the chicken and then leave to marinate for 1 hour.

Remove the stalks and seeds from the peppers and slice the flesh into fine strips. Halve the onion and cut into thin half-moons and then crush the garlic. Trim the spring onions and finely chop along with the coriander.

Pour the oil into a large heavy-based frying pan and, when the oil is hot, add the onion and gently fry over a low–medium heat for about 15 minutes or until soft and just starting to caramelise. Add the peppers, garlic and lime juice to the pan, increase the heat slightly and cook for another 2 minutes.

Add the chicken with the marinade and fry for a further 5 minutes, stirring regularly, until the meat is tender and just cooked through. Add a dash of the apple juice to the cornflour and stir to a smooth paste. Pour the remaining apple juice over the chicken, add the cornflour mixture and allow to simmer, stirring frequently, for another minute or until the sauce thickens. Scatter over the spring onions and coriander to serve

lemon &
ginger chicken

nut-free option

This Chinese-style sweet-sharp dish is both wonderfully fragrant and incredibly simple to prepare. The green peppers add a delicate bite to the citrus-imbued chicken, while the ginger gives a warming note enhanced by the spicy heat of the chilli. Serve with a bowl of basmati rice and perhaps a few roasted cashews scattered over the top. Alternatively, you could make it into an oriental feast by serving it alongside my Stir-fry Jasmine Rice and Sweet and Sour Chicken or Sweet Chilli and Sesame Salmon (see pages 191, 189 and 150).

contains nuts   *nut-free option*   *gluten free*   *dairy free*   *egg free*   *soya free*   *yeast free*

Serves 4

5cm piece of root ginger
5 cloves of garlic
2 green peppers
8 skinless and boneless chicken thighs or 4 skinless chicken breasts
60ml toasted sesame oil (or smoked rapeseed oil for a nut-free option)
1 tsp Chinese five-spice powder
125ml chicken or vegetable stock (see the Glossary, page 232)
125ml lemon juice
2 tbsp golden caster sugar
1 tsp cornflour mixed with 1 tbsp water
1 fresh red chilli

Finely grate both the ginger and the garlic. Remove the stalks and seeds from the peppers and cut the flesh into 2cm-thick lengths. Slice the chicken into bite-sized pieces.

Heat half of the sesame or rapeseed oil in a large wok or frying pan until very hot. Add the chicken and the peppers to the pan and fry over a medium–high heat for about 3 minutes or until the chicken is sealed and just starting to brown on the outside. Add the garlic, ginger and five-spice powder and continue to fry for a further minute.

Pour over the remaining oil, followed by the stock and lemon juice, and bring to the boil. Reduce the heat and leave to simmer gently for 10 minutes, then stir in the sugar and the cornflour mixture and cook for a further 5 minutes. Finely slice the red chilli into rounds (retaining the seeds) and scatter over the chicken before serving.

stir-fry
jasmine rice

This colourful stir-fry is one of those recipes that's rather more than the sum of its parts. The ingredients may look basic, but with a little tweaking you end up with an exciting and delicious dish. The trick here is to add the remaining ginger, coriander and spring onions right at the very end of cooking; a simple step, but it adds a fresh vibrancy to the dish and makes a notable difference. You can serve it as it is for a simple supper, with perhaps a few roasted cashew nuts scattered over, or it makes a wonderful accompaniment to my Sweet Chilli and Sesame Salmon (see page 150). Served alongside my Lemon and Ginger Chicken and Sweet and Sour Chicken (see pages 190 and 189), it would make a real feast.

nut free   *gluten free*   *vegan*   *soya free*   *yeast free*

Serves 4

175g jasmine rice
A pinch of sea salt flakes
Grated zest and juice of
   1 lemon
2 cloves of garlic
5cm piece of root ginger
6 spring onions
A small bunch of coriander
3 peppers (any colour except
   green)
150g frozen peas
2 tbsp sunflower or olive oil

Place the jasmine rice in a large saucepan along with the salt, lemon zest and juice and 500ml of water. Cover with a lid and bring to the boil, then reduce the heat and leave to simmer gently for around 10 minutes or until the rice has absorbed all of the liquid. Set aside to cool down.

Grate the garlic and half the root ginger into a mixing bowl. Trim the spring onions and finely slice into rounds, setting aside the chopped green sections with the remaining ginger. Finely chop the coriander, reserving the chopped leaves to add later, then add the chopped stalks and the white rounds of the spring onions to the mixing bowl.

Remove the stalks and seeds from the peppers and slice the flesh into strips about 5mm thick. Cover the peas in boiling water, leave for 5 minutes and then drain.

Next, heat the sunflower or olive oil in a large wok or frying pan. When the oil is hot, add the contents of the mixing bowl and the peppers to the pan and stir-fry over a medium–high heat for 8–10 minutes or until the peppers are just starting to soften.

Add the cooked rice and peas to the pan and continue to stir-fry for a further 5 minutes. Finally, grate in the remaining ginger and add the chopped coriander leaves and the green parts of the spring onions to the rice. Stir through and then serve while hot.

lamb burgers
with beetroot hummus

nut-free option

Tasty lamb burgers, lightly spiced, are topped with a sweet and sultry beetroot hummus – the combination works really well and makes an ideal weekend supper. I recommend first cooking a big batch of quinoa – enough for the hummus and to make into my Quinoa Tabbouleh (see page 66) to accompany the burgers. I also like to take whole leaves from an iceberg lettuce to create a vegetable 'bun' for each burger. Simply sit the burger inside, add a spoonful of hummus, and perhaps a little chopped tomato or onion, and enjoy!

contains nuts   *nut-free option*   *gluten free*   *dairy free*   *egg free*   *soya free*   *yeast free*

Makes 4 burgers

For the burgers
1 small red onion
1 clove of garlic
500g lean minced lamb
½ tsp chilli flakes
½ tsp ground coriander
¼ tsp dried mint
½ tsp sea salt flakes
1 tbsp olive oil, for frying

For the beetroot hummus
1 tsp cumin seeds
½ clove of garlic
75g cooked quinoa or
   cooked rice
2–3 cooked beetroots
1 tbsp tahini (or sunflower
   seed butter for a nut-free
   option – see the Glossary,
   pages 232–3)
1–2 tbsp extra-virgin olive oil
Juice of 1 lemon
Sea salt flakes and freshly
   ground black pepper

Finely chop the onion and crush the garlic, then place all the ingredients for the burgers, except for the olive oil, in a large mixing bowl and mush together with your hands until combined. Divide the mixture into four and shape into 2cm-thick patties, then set aside until ready to cook.

Next, make the hummus. Place the cumin seeds in a small heavy-based frying pan and dry-fry over a medium heat for 1 minute or until lightly toasted and fragrant. Place in a mortar and grind with a pestle into a fine powder. Alternatively, place in a freezer bag and crush with a rolling pin.

Crush the garlic and then place in a food processor with the ground cumin and all the other ingredients and blitz until completely smooth, stopping every now and then to scrape down the sides of the bowl. Season with salt and pepper to taste and add a little extra olive oil or lemon juice if necessary.

Heat the olive oil in a large non-stick frying pan, then add the burgers and fry over a medium–high heat for around 4 minutes on each side or until cooked to your liking. Serve the burgers with a generous dollop of beetroot hummus on top.

spicy bean burgers
with avocado salsa

These little burgers make such a great summery dish; indeed, they would be lovely cooked outside on a barbecue. As with my Lamb Burgers (see page 192), I like to use the outer leaves of an iceberg lettuce to wrap around these like a crisp green 'bun'. That way you can add the salsa and perhaps a little hummus (see page 173) to make a real feast of it. It's really important that you grate the carrot and courgette by hand, as using a food processor can make them very soggy.

contains nuts   nut-free option   gluten free   vegan   soya free   yeast free

Makes 10 burgers

For the burgers
1 large red onion
2 cloves of garlic
2 courgettes
2 carrots
A small bunch of coriander
2 tbsp olive oil
2 tbsp crunchy peanut butter
(or sunflower seed butter
for a nut-free option –
see the Glossary,
pages 232–3)
1 tbsp harissa paste
1 x 400g tin of kidney beans,
dried and rinsed
100g cooked rice
50g sesame seeds (or
polenta for a nut-free
option)

For the avocado salsa
2 tomatoes
½ small red onion
1 fresh red chilli
1 large ripe avocado
(preferably Hass)
½ yellow pepper
Juice of 2 limes
A small bunch of coriander
Sea salt flakes and freshly
ground black pepper

First, make the avocado salsa. Place the tomatoes in a bowl and cover with boiling water, then leave for 1 minute. Drain the water off and gently peel the skin from the tomatoes with a small sharp knife. Cut the tomatoes in half and, using a teaspoon, scoop out the seeds and discard. Set the remaining tomato flesh aside.

Finely dice the onion, then deseed the chilli and chop very finely. Halve the avocado, discard the stone, scoop out the flesh with a spoon and finely chop. Slice the tomato flesh and yellow pepper into very small dice and then combine all of the ingredients in a bowl. Pour over the lime juice, then finely chop the coriander and stir in. Season with salt and pepper to taste, cover with a plate or cling film and leave to stand in the fridge until ready to use. (The salsa will keep, covered, in the fridge for 48 hours, though the avocado may discolour.)

Next, prepare the burgers. Finely chop the onion and crush the garlic. Trim the ends from the courgettes and carrots and then coarsely grate by hand. Finely chop the coriander and set aside.

Heat 1 tablespoon of the olive oil in a large frying pan, add the onion and fry gently over a low–medium heat for around 5 minutes or until softened and lightly caramelised at the edges. Add the garlic, courgettes and carrots to the pan, increase the heat to medium–high and fry for a further 5 minutes, stirring regularly, until the carrots and courgettes have softened.

continues...

spicy bean burgers
with avocado salsa

Add the peanut butter (or sunflower seed butter) and harissa paste to the pan, season well with salt and pepper and continue to cook for 3 minutes, stirring regularly, until blended with the vegetables. Take off the heat and leave to stand for 5 minutes or until cool enough to handle.

Meanwhile, place the kidney beans in a food processor and blitz into a smooth paste before transferring to a large mixing bowl. Alternatively, place the kidney beans in a mixing bowl and mash by hand, using a fork, until you have a thick paste.

Add the cooked rice, vegetable mixture and chopped coriander to the mashed beans and beat together until combined and forming a large ball. Take a handful of the mixture – about 3 tablespoons – and shape into a patty approximately 5cm in diameter and 2.5cm thick. Scatter the sesame seeds (or polenta) over a flat plate and season with salt and pepper, then lightly roll the burgers in the seeds (or polenta) so that they are evenly coated. Cover the burgers in cling film and chill in the fridge for 1 hour before cooking.

When ready to cook, heat the remaining olive oil in a large frying pan and fry the burgers for about 10 minutes, turning over once or twice, until golden brown and cooked through.

herb-crusted rack of lamb with sloe gin gravy & butter bean mash

The major advantage of roasting a rack of lamb – here cooked with a crisp herbed crust to offset the rich and succulent meat – is that it offers maximum impact for minimum input. All you have to do is pop it in the oven, then prepare the mash (virtually instant, as it uses tinned butter beans) and pull together the gravy at the end, making it ideal for a relaxed supper with friends or a celebratory lunch. To make it into an even bigger treat, you could serve it with roast potatoes, green beans and caramelised peas and carrots – all the trimmings for a restorative feast.

nut free   *gluten free*   *dairy free*   *egg free*   *soya free*   *yeast free*

Serves 6

2 large racks of lamb (about 8 ribs each)
1 red onion
4 cloves of garlic
Leaves from a small bunch of rosemary
A small bunch of flat-leaf parsley
3 tbsp dairy-free margarine
2 tbsp olive oil
200g allergen-free breadcrumbs (such as from leftover Socca or Chickpea Bread – see pages 71 and 28)
2 tsp redcurrant jelly
Sea salt flakes and freshly ground black pepper

For the bean mash
1 bulb of garlic
2 x 400g tins of cannellini beans, drained and rinsed
1 tbsp olive oil

For the gravy
2 tbsp sloe gin
300ml hot chicken or vegetable stock (see the Glossary, page 232)
1½ tbsp cornflour mixed with 1½ tbsp water

Preheat the oven to 200°C (400°F), gas mark 6.

Trim the lamb of any obvious excess fat (or ask your butcher to do this for you), then leave the meat out to come up to room temperature while you prepare the rest of the dish.

Wrap the garlic bulb for the bean mash in foil and bake in the oven for 20 minutes or until soft.

Meanwhile, make the herb crust. Finely dice the onion and crush the 4 cloves of garlic. Finely chop the fresh herbs. Place the margarine and olive oil in a saucepan and gently melt together. Add the onion and garlic and fry gently over a low heat for 10 minutes or until completely softened but not browned. Once softened, add the breadcrumbs and fry together for a minute or until the breadcrumbs have absorbed the oil. Add the redcurrant jelly and stir together until the jelly has melted into the mixture. Remove from the heat, season well with salt and pepper and stir in the chopped herbs.

Place the racks of lamb in a large roasting tin, meat-side down with the ribs interlocking. Firmly press the herb crumb over the exterior, fatty side of the lamb until evenly covered. Place in the oven and roast for 25–30 minutes (25 minutes for lightly pink lamb, 30 minutes for a more medium roast).

continues...

herb-crusted rack of lamb with sloe gin gravy & butter bean mash

While the lamb is cooking, continue with the bean mash. Place the cannellini beans in a saucepan. Cover with water and bring to the boil, then reduce the heat and leave to simmer for 10 minutes. Drain the beans and then return to the saucepan. Next, unwrap the baked garlic bulb and squeeze the soft cloves out of their skins into the pan. Pour in the olive oil and mash coarsely with a potato masher or fork, seasoning with salt and pepper to taste.

Remove the lamb from the oven, transfer to a board and cover in foil, leaving to rest for 15 minutes. Meanwhile, to make the gravy, place the roasting tin with the juices from the lamb over a medium heat. Add the sloe gin and deglaze the pan, scraping up any gooey bits, then pour in the hot stock and bring to a gentle simmer. Add the cornflour mixture to the simmering stock, a little at a time and whisking continuously, until you have the desired consistency for your gravy.

Heat the bean mash through and serve together with the herb-crusted lamb and hot gravy.

For an alternative to the bean mash, steam 500g of peeled and chopped parsnips until soft. Place in a food processor with a dash of dairy-free milk and knob of dairy-free margerine. Season and blitz until you have a velvety puree...

Proper Puddings

lemon tart
vanilla ice cream
apple &
blackberry pie
mango &
pineapple puddings
strawberry ice cream
chocolate ice cream
chocolate &
coconut crunch
gooseberry & redcurrant woodland
crumble with vanilla custard
decadent chocolate tart
french apple tart
rhubarb &
ginger sponge
gooey
chocolate pudding
baked
syrup sponge
pumpkin pudding
with spiced toffee sauce

lemon tart

Bright, zesty and delicious, this lemon tart is perfect for serving in the warmer months. I love the intense citrus flavours that come from combining the lemony pastry, flecked with zest, and the unctuous yet tangy filling.

contains nuts   nut-free option   gluten free   vegan   soya free   yeast free

Serves 12

For the lemon
shortcrust pastry
230g gluten-free plain flour
   (ideally Doves Farm)
½ tsp xanthan gum
60g vegetable shortening
60g dairy-free margarine
Grated zest of 1 lemon
2 tbsp golden caster sugar
1 tbsp lemon juice

For the filling
3 tbsp agar agar flakes
150g golden caster sugar
160ml lemon juice (about
   6 lemons)
Grated zest of 2 lemons
3 tbsp cornflour
60ml almond milk (or rice milk
   for a nut-free option)

Equipment
You will need a 20cm round
   tart tin with a removable
   base for this recipe

Preheat the oven to 200°C (400°F), gas mark 6.

Sift the flour and xanthan gum into the bowl of a food processor. Cut the vegetable shortening into cubes and add to the flour with the margarine. Pulse until the mixture is of a breadcrumb-like consistency. Add the lemon zest and caster sugar and pulse for another minute. Alternatively, place the ingredients in a large mixing bowl and rub together with your fingertips.

Tip in the lemon juice and 1 tablespoon of cold water, pulsing as you go (or stirring with a flat-bladed knife if making the pastry by hand), until the mixture begins to pull together to form a dough. You can then add an extra tablespoon of water if you think it needs it. Turn the pastry into a large mixing bowl (or keep in the same bowl, if making by hand) and, using your fingertips, pull together into a ball. Knead lightly for about 2 minutes or until smooth and elastic to the touch.

Shape the pastry into a ball and place between two large sheets of cling film. Gently roll it out into a circle slightly larger than the tart tin and no thinner than 3mm. Peel off the uppermost sheet of cling film and carefully turn the pastry into the tin, filling in any cracks or gaps with extra pastry patted flat with your fingertips, and then trim the edges.

Cover the pastry with a layer of baking parchment and fill with baking beans, then blind bake for 15 minutes. Remove the paper and beans and return to the oven for another 10 minutes or until the pastry is cooked through and lightly golden. Remove from the oven and set aside to cool down while you make the filling for the tart.

continues...

lemon tart

Place the agar agar flakes in a high-sided saucepan filled with 330ml of water. Bring to the boil and leave to bubble gently for about 10 minutes, whisking every now and then, until the agar agar has dissolved. (Don't worry if the liquid foams up – this is normal and explains why you need a deep pan.) Add the sugar to the liquid and continue to boil gently, whisking occasionally, for 3–4 minutes or until the sugar has dissolved into the liquid, then remove from the heat.

In a separate bowl, combine the lemon juice, zest and cornflour and stir together until smooth. Add this mixture and the almond (or rice) milk to the agar agar liquid and whisk together constantly, over a medium heat, for around 5 minutes or until the mixture thickens and becomes syrupy. Take off the heat and set aside to cool for a few minutes.

Pour the lemon filling into the tart case, leave to cool at room temperature for 30 minutes and then place in the fridge to set for 1 hour before serving.

nut-free
option

vanilla
ice cream

Everyone loves ice cream, and this intolerance-friendly recipe is so good that you'll be wanting to make it all the time! Here, I've adopted the Sicilian tradition of using cornflour rather than eggs to thicken the mixture; it makes for a slightly lighter ice cream, but the dairy-free milk keeps things creamy. For the record, I favour using almond milk for the creamiest results, although you could use coconut milk (from a carton rather than a tin) or rice milk for a nut-free option. It really is heavenly and goes beautifully with all manner of things: Gooseberry and Redcurrant Woodland Crumble, Pumpkin Pudding, Apple Pancakes with Cinnamon-Roasted Fruit (see pages 213, 222 and 24), to name but a few. I like to use vanilla bean paste for its depth of flavour and the nice speckled appearance it gives the ice cream.

contains nuts   *nut-free option*   *gluten free*   *vegan*   *soya free*   *yeast free*

Serves 4

450ml almond milk (or
    coconut or rice milk
    for a nut-free option)
15g cornflour
75g golden caster sugar
1 tbsp vanilla bean paste

Equipment
You will need an ice-cream
    maker (minimum capacity
    of 1 litre) for this recipe

In a small bowl or jug, add 100ml of the almond (or coconut or rice) milk to the cornflour and stir together until smooth.

Place the caster sugar in a large mixing bowl. Pour the remaining milk into a saucepan and add the vanilla bean paste, then heat gently until just simmering. Take the pan off the heat and pour the milk over the sugar, whisking as you go to dissolve the sugar and keep the mixture smooth.

Return the mixture to the saucepan and place back on the hob, then whisk in the cornflour mixture and leave to simmer gently for 2–3 minutes, whisking all the time, until smooth and slightly thickened.

Pour the mixture into a clean bowl or jug and leave to cool at room temperature for 1 hour. After an hour, whisk the mixture, cover with cling film and then chill in the fridge for 2–24 hours. (The longer you chill the ice cream the better the results will be when you churn it in the ice-cream maker and there is less chance of ice crystals forming in the finished ice cream.) Once chilled, freeze and churn in an ice-cream maker according to the manufacturer's directions.

apple &
blackberry pie

Apple pie is the kind of dish that provides exactly what's needed for a particular occasion, whether to celebrate, commiserate or to comfort. An easy and joyous thing to bake, filling your home with its sugar-crusted fragrance, it's also simply delicious. Serve warm or cold with a generous scoop of Vanilla Ice Cream (see page 205) for a decadent dessert, or just with a cup of tea for an afternoon treat.

nut free   gluten free   vegan   soya free   yeast free

Serves 8 generously

For the shortcrust pastry
350g gluten-free plain flour
    (ideally Doves Farm)
¾ tsp xanthan gum
75g vegetable shortening
75g dairy-free margarine
3 tbsp golden caster sugar,
    plus extra for sprinkling

For the filling
3–4 Bramley apples
150g blackberries
4 tbsp golden caster sugar

Equipment
You will need a 23cm round
    pie dish, about 5cm deep,
    for this recipe

Preheat the oven to 190°C (375°F), gas mark 5.

Sift the flour and xanthan gum into the bowl of a food processor. Cut the vegetable shortening into cubes and add to the flour with the margarine and sugar, then pulse until the mixture is of a breadcrumb-like consistency. Alternatively, place the ingredients in a large mixing bowl and rub together with your fingertips.

Add 3 tablespoons of cold water, pulsing as you go (or stirring with a flat-bladed knife if making the pastry by hand), until the mixture begins to pull together to form a dough. You can then add an extra tablespoon of water if you think it needs it. Turn the pastry into a large mixing bowl (or keep in the same bowl, if making by hand) and, using your fingertips, pull together into a ball. Knead lightly for about 2 minutes or until smooth and elastic to the touch.

Separate the pastry into two portions, one comprising two-thirds of the dough. Place the larger of the pastry balls between two sheets of cling film and roll into a circle roughly the same diameter as the pie dish and no thinner than 3mm. Peel off the uppermost sheet of cling film, lay your pie dish over the pastry and run a sharp knife around the edge of the dish to cut the pastry into a perfect circle. Using the bottom sheet of cling film as a lever, carefully lay the pastry in the base of the pie dish, removing the cling film and filling any cracks or gaps with a little extra pastry, patted flat with your fingertips.

Ball up a little of the excess pastry and roll into a thin sausage about 1cm thick. Lay the 'sausage' of pastry around the edge of the pie dish, lightly pressing it into the rim of the existing pastry to form a ridge. Add any excess to the remaining ball of dough, then place between two fresh sheets of cling film (it will roll better this way) and roll into another circle, slightly wider in diameter than the pie dish, for the pastry top. Set aside while you make the filling.

Peel and core the apples, then slice into 3mm-thick segments and place in the pastry-lined pie dish, piling the apples high and scattering over the blackberries and sugar as you go. Cover the top of the pie with the remaining pastry circle and press into the pie rim, crimping and sealing as you go. Run a sharp knife around the edge of the pie, trimming off any excess pastry. You can then re-roll this and cut it into shapes of your choice to decorate the top of the pie.

To allow the steam to escape during cooking, make four small cuts in the centre of the pie (each about 1cm long, almost like a star but not joining in the middle) and bake for 40–45 minutes or until fragrant and lightly golden. Remove from the oven and scatter with sugar, then leave for 20 minutes and serve warm or allow to cool down completely.

proper puddings

mango &
pineapple puddings

Bright and fruity, these little puddings are delicious and delightfully easy to make. They have the appearance of jelly but a creamy, fool-like consistency – created by using agar agar flakes (see the Glossary, page 224). The result is a wonderfully summery dessert that provides the perfect refreshing end to a meal.

nut free   gluten free   vegan   soya free   yeast free

Serves 8

200g fresh or tinned
    pineapple slices
1 litre mango juice
Juice of ½ lemon
3 heaped tbsp agar agar
    flakes

Equipment
You will need 8 ramekins or
    glasses for this recipe

Cut the pineapple into 5mm dice. Combine the mango and lemon juice in a large saucepan and place over a medium heat. When the liquid is hot but not simmering, add the agar agar flakes and bring to the boil. Reduce the heat and leave to simmer for 10–15 minutes, stirring regularly, until the agar agar has dissolved completely.

Remove from the heat and then pour into the ramekins or glasses. Divide the pineapple pieces equally between the ramekins or glasses and allow to cool down to room temperature – they will be semi-set at this point. Transfer the puddings to the fridge and leave, uncovered, for at least 1 hour to set completely.

strawberry
ice cream

nut-free
option

Glorious, fresh and simple, this ice cream is best made when strawberries are really in season – you'll taste the difference and find yourself with an ambrosial treat. I like to make my ice cream with almond milk as I think it gives the creamiest results, but coconut milk (from a carton rather than the tinned variety) or rice milk would also work well. Serve with fresh strawberries, blueberries and raspberries for a delicious summertime pudding.

contains nuts   *nut-free option*   *gluten free*   *vegan*   *soya free*   *yeast free*

Serves 4

450ml almond milk (or
    coconut or rice milk
    for a nut-free option)
15g cornflour
75g golden caster sugar
¼ tsp vanilla extract
400g fresh strawberries

Equipment
You will need an ice-cream
    maker (minimum capacity
    of 1 litre) for this recipe

In a small bowl or jug, add 100ml of the almond (or coconut or rice) milk to the cornflour and stir together until smooth.

Place the caster sugar in a large mixing bowl and add the vanilla extract. Pour the remaining milk into a saucepan and heat gently until just simmering. Take the pan off the heat and pour the milk over the sugar, whisking as you go to dissolve the sugar and keep the mixture smooth.

Return the mixture to the saucepan and place back on the hob, then whisk in the cornflour mixture and leave to simmer gently for 2–3 minutes, whisking all the time, until smooth and slightly thickened.

Pour the mixture into a clean bowl or jug and leave to cool at room temperature for 1 hour.

Meanwhile, hull the strawberries and blitz to a purée in a food processor. Stir into the ice-cream mixture, then cover with cling film and chill in the fridge for 2–24 hours. (The longer you chill the ice cream the better the results will be when you churn it in the ice-cream maker and there is less chance of ice crystals forming in the finished ice cream.) Once chilled, freeze and churn in an ice-cream maker according to the manufacturer's directions.

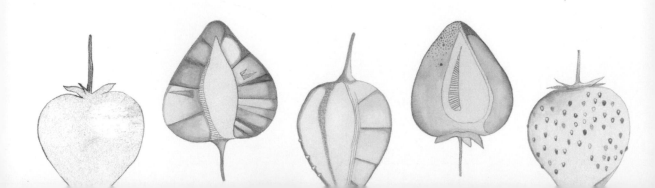

chocolate ice cream

Rich, intense and decidedly chocolaty, this ice cream is again made following the Sicilian method of using cornflour rather than eggs to thicken the mixture; it makes for a velvety affair, deep and creamy and absolutely delicious. Serve on its own with rich red berries or with a slice of Gingerbread Loaf (see page 106) for a truly decadent pudding. A word about the coconut milk used here: I don't mean the tins of very thick coconut milk used in cooking, but rather the cartons of slightly thinner pouring milk (see the Glossary, page 227).

contains nuts　　*nut-free option*　　*gluten free*　　*vegan*　　*soya free*　　*yeast free*

Serves 4

450ml almond milk (or coconut or rice milk for a nut-free option)
15g cornflour
75g golden caster sugar
50g cocoa powder

Equipment
You will need an ice-cream maker (minimum capacity of 1 litre) for this recipe

In a small bowl or jug, add 100ml of the almond (or coconut or rice) milk to the cornflour and stir together until smooth.

Place the caster sugar and cocoa powder in a large mixing bowl. Pour the remaining milk into a saucepan and heat gently until just simmering. Take the pan off the heat and pour the milk over the sugar and cocoa powder, whisking as you go to dissolve the sugar and keep the mixture smooth.

Return the mixture to the saucepan and place back on the hob, then whisk in the cornflour mixture and leave to simmer gently for 2–3 minutes, whisking all the time, until smooth and slightly thickened.

Pour the mixture into a clean bowl or jug and leave to cool at room temperature for 1 hour. After an hour, whisk the mixture, cover with cling film and then chill in the fridge for 2–24 hours. (The longer you chill the ice cream the better the results will be when you churn it in the ice-cream maker and there is less chance of ice crystals forming in the finished ice cream.) Once chilled, freeze and churn in an ice-cream maker according to the manufacturer's directions.

chocolate &
coconut crunch

Chocolate crunch is traditionally made with copious amounts of butter and lard, so not the healthiest choice for a children's treat – especially when smothered in a synthetic pink sauce, as it was at my primary school! This uses coconut oil instead, giving all the flavour and 'crunch' of the original but in a much healthier way. Children love it, especially when served with a pouring of chocolate custard (you can adapt my vanilla custard recipe on page 213, adding 1 heaped tablespoon of cocoa powder to the rice milk along with the sugar); it's just the sort of thing that childhood memories are made of. If stored in an airtight container, it will keep for up to three days.

nut free   *gluten free*   *vegan*   *soya free*   *yeast free*

Serves 15

4 tbsp ground flaxseed
¼ tsp gluten-free baking
  powder
250g coconut oil (in a
  solid state at room
  temperature), plus
  extra for greasing
500g gluten-free self-raising
  flour (ideally Doves Farm)
50g cocoa powder
200g golden caster sugar,
  plus 1 tbsp for sprinkling

Equipment
You will need an 18cm x 25cm
  baking tin for this recipe

Preheat the oven to 150°C (300°F), gas mark 2, then grease the baking tin with coconut oil and line with baking parchment.

Place the flaxseed and baking powder in a small bowl, add 6 tablespoons of water and stir together. Leave to thicken while you prepare the remaining ingredients.

Place the coconut oil in a small saucepan and melt over a low heat. Sift the flour and cocoa powder into a large mixing bowl and add the sugar. Spoon in the flaxseed mixture and pour over the melted coconut oil, then stir together into a thick, evenly mixed dough.

Press the dough into the baking tin, ensuring that it is evenly spread. Bake in the oven for 55–60 minutes or until the mixture is firm to the touch. Remove from the oven, sprinkle over the remaining sugar and leave to cool in the tin before cutting into squares to serve.

gooseberry & redcurrant woodland crumble with vanilla custard

More often associated with jams and jellies, gooseberries and redcurrants seem a little overlooked these days when it comes to puddings. Put almost any type of fruit in a crumble, however, and it shows it to delicious advantage, and this version of the dish is particularly yummy. Here, the gooseberries and redcurrants make for rich and slightly tart bedfellows, while the addition of soft dark brown sugar to the crumble topping gives a lovely mellow note that really complements the fruit. The custard sets the crumble off beautifully, although a scoop of Vanilla Ice Cream (see page 205) would go equally well.

nut free   gluten free   vegan   soya free   yeast free

Serves 6

For the filling
500g fresh gooseberries
250g fresh redcurrants
2 tbsp golden caster sugar
2 tbsp apple juice

For the crumble topping
225g gluten-free plain flour
    (ideally Doves Farm)
115g soft dark brown sugar
115g dairy-free margarine

For the custard
600ml rice milk
3 tbsp golden caster sugar
2 tsp vanilla extract
2 tbsp cornflour mixed with
    2 tbsp water
A very small pinch of
    turmeric, for colouring
    (optional)

Equipment
You will need a baking dish
    measuring about 15cm x
    23cm for this recipe

Preheat the oven to 180°C (350°F), gas mark 4.

First, prepare the fruit for the filling. Top and tail the gooseberries and redcurrants and mix together in the baking dish. Scatter over the caster sugar and pour over the apple juice.

To make the crumble topping, sift the flour into a mixing bowl and add the brown sugar, then use your fingertips to rub in the margarine until the mixture is of a breadcrumb-like consistency. Spread the crumble topping over the fruit and bake in the oven for 35 minutes or until golden and bubbling.

While the crumble is cooking, make the custard. Heat the rice milk in a saucepan until just simmering but not boiling, then whisk in the sugar and vanilla extract until dissolved. Add the cornflour mixture and whisk the custard in the pan until it reaches the desired consistency. Add the turmeric (if using) and whisk into the custard, then pour over the warm crumble to serve.

decadent
chocolate tart

nut-free option

Despite being the most luxurious of chocolate tarts, this dessert is relatively good for you. Using the purest of raw ingredients, it makes for the most delectable pudding and is so rich and intensely flavoured that a little goes a long way. The idea comes from the raw-food movement, currently growing in popularity, although I have to admit that this particular tart is not 100 per cent raw. The addition of cocoa powder and maple syrup means that you couldn't serve this to a staunch raw foodist. But not to worry; you can get hold of the raw stuff instead, or simply serve it to a bunch of 'heat eaters', as I do, to see the look of sheer pleasure on each of their faces as they take the first bite.

contains nuts   *nut-free option*   *gluten free*   *vegan*   *soya free*   *yeast free*

Serves 12

For the tart base
120g shelled walnuts and pecans (or sunflower seeds for a nut-free option)
100g desiccated coconut
2 tbsp cocoa powder
150g pitted dates (preferably Medjool)
A pinch of sea salt flakes

For the chocolate filling
160g cocoa powder
500ml maple syrup
210g coconut oil (in a solid state at room temperature)

Equipment
You will need a 20cm round cake tin with a removable base for this recipe

First, line the cake tin with a sheet of cling film, laying it as smoothly as possible inside the tin. Next, place the walnuts and pecans (or sunflower seeds) in a food processor, add the desiccated coconut and cocoa powder and pulse until the mixture is the consistency of fine breadcrumbs.

Add the dates and the pinch of sea salt and continue to pulse, then add 50ml of water, pulsing as you go, until the mixture combines and pulls together. Add more water (up to 30ml) to help bind the mixture if it isn't holding together.

Transfer the mixture to the prepared cake tin, pressing down lightly with your fingers to spread it over the bottom of the tin. Then, using the back of a spoon, smooth out the mixture so that it forms an even base for the tart. Place in the fridge and leave to chill while you make the filling.

Place the cocoa powder, maple syrup and coconut oil in a blender or food processor. (I recommend using a high-powered blender instead of a food processor, as it will give you a creamier result.) Blitz the ingredients until you have a completely smooth, creamy filling – this may take a few minutes.

Pour the chocolate filling over the base of the tart, level the top with the back of a spoon and then chill in the fridge for at least 3 hours before serving. A little tip: when ready to serve, run a large knife under the hot tap before slicing the tart, repeating for every slice, as this will give you the smoothest cut.

french
apple tart

Crisp pastry covered in a thick layer of apple purée, this tart is a delight to the senses with its sweet fragrance and light texture. I like to serve it warm with a scoop of Vanilla Ice Cream (see page 205) sprinkled with cinnamon, although it is equally lovely when left to cool and then served with a pot of tea. Once you've puréed the apples, be sure to collect the wonderfully sweet apple syrup that is drained off. Mixed with a litre of sparkling water, it makes the most heavenly and refreshing drink – an added bonus to making the dish.

nut free   gluten free   vegan   soya free   yeast free

Serves 6–8

For the shortcrust pastry
230g gluten-free plain flour
   (ideally Doves Farm)
½ tsp xanthan gum
60g vegetable shortening
60g dairy-free margarine
2 tbsp caster sugar

For the apple filling
900g Bramley apples
150g golden caster sugar
1 eating apple
1 tbsp apricot jam

Equipment
You will need a 23cm round
   tart tin with a removable
   base for this recipe

Begin by making the apple purée. Peel and core the Bramley apples and chop into chunks roughly 2cm in size. Place in a saucepan with the caster sugar and 2 tablespoons of water. Heat gently, stirring every now and then, until completely softened and stewed. Remove from the heat, leave to cool for about 5 minutes and then beat with a wooden spoon until smooth. Tip the purée into a fine-mesh sieve, with a bowl underneath to catch the juice, and leave for about 20 minutes to drain and cool.

Preheat the oven to 200°C (400°F), gas mark 6.

Sift the flour and xanthan gum into the bowl of a food processor. Cut the vegetable shortening into cubes and add to the flour with the margarine and sugar, then pulse until the mixture is of a breadcrumb-like consistency. Alternatively, place the ingredients in a large mixing bowl and rub together with your fingertips.

Add 2 tablespoons of cold water, pulsing as you go (or stirring with a flat-bladed knife, if making the pastry by hand), until the mixture begins to pull together to form a dough. You can then add an extra tablespoon of water if you think it needs it.

Turn the pastry into a large mixing bowl (or keep in the same bowl, if making by hand) and, using your fingertips, pull together into a ball. Knead lightly for 2 minutes or until smooth and elastic to the touch.

Shape the pastry into a ball and place between two large sheets of cling film. Gently roll it out into a circle slightly larger than the tart tin and no thinner than 3mm. Peel off the uppermost sheet of cling film and carefully turn the pastry into the tin, peeling off the bottom layer of cling film.

continues...

Gently fit the pastry into the tin, trimming the edges with a sharp knife and filling in any cracks or gaps with extra pastry, patted flat with your fingertips.

Carefully tip the apple purée into the tart case and spread out evenly, smoothing the top with the back of a spoon.

Peel and core the eating apple and finely slice into thin segments. Working quickly before the apple slices go brown, arrange them around the outer edge of the tart to form a decorative circle, each segment slightly overlapping the last one. Use 4–5 smaller slivers of apple to form a smaller fan in the centre of the tart and then bake in the oven for 30 minutes or until the apples have browned slightly and the pastry is crisp.

Remove from the oven and place on a wire rack to cool down a little. Heat the apricot jam in a small saucepan until melted and then brush over the top of the tart to finish.

rhubarb &
ginger sponge

Ideal for making when rhubarb is in season, this is a wonderfully homely pudding, the sweet-sour tang of the fruit offset by the touch of ginger and the light sponge topping. You can easily substitute in other combinations of fruit if you prefer: gooseberries with elderflower cordial, for instance, or apple and blackberry or peach and raspberry. Serve with custard or a generous dollop of Vanilla Ice Cream (see pages 213 and 205) – delicious!

nut free   gluten free   vegan   soya free   yeast free

Serves 6–8

For the fruit filling
6 sticks of rhubarb
5mm piece of root ginger
2 tbsp golden caster sugar
1 tbsp orange juice or water

For the sponge topping
115g dairy-free margarine
115g golden caster sugar,
    plus 1 tbsp for sprinkling
2 heaped tsp egg replacer
    (ideally Orgran) whisked
    with 4 tbsp water
225g gluten-free self-raising
    flour (ideally Doves Farm)
4 tbsp rice or other dairy-
    free milk

Equipment
You will need a 13cm x 20cm
    baking dish, about 5cm
    deep, for this recipe

Preheat the oven to 180°C (350°F), gas mark 4.

Begin by preparing the fruit filling. Trim the rhubarb and chop into 2cm chunks, then place in the baking dish. Finely grate the ginger over the rhubarb, sprinkle over the sugar and pour in the orange juice or water. Set aside while you make the sponge topping.

Place the margarine and caster sugar in a large mixing bowl and, using a wooden spoon, cream together until combined. Add the egg replacer mixture, a little at a time and stirring as you go until fully incorporated. (Don't worry if the mixture splits at this point; the flour will pull it back together.) Sift in the flour, pour over the rice milk and fold them into the mixture with a metal spoon.

Dollop the sponge mixture over the top of the fruit in an even layer. (It's best to spoon it on in blobs, working in a spiral from the outside to the centre of the dish, then smooth over the top with the back of the spoon.) Sprinkle with sugar and bake in the oven for around 45 minutes or until golden and slightly crisp. Serve warm from the oven.

gooey chocolate pudding

Rich, decadent and ludicrously chocolaty, this dish is one of those uncomplicated English classics – a self-saucing sponge. Using simple store-cupboard ingredients, you can produce a gloriously gooey pudding that will be adored by children and adults alike. It's true comfort food and is made to be shared.

contains nuts   nut-free option   gluten free   vegan   soya free   yeast free

Serves 6–8

4 tbsp ground flaxseed
125g gluten-free plain flour (ideally Doves Farm)
3 heaped tsp gluten-free baking powder
6 tbsp cocoa powder
120g golden caster sugar
A small pinch of sea salt flakes
100ml rice milk
150ml almond milk (or coconut milk for a nut-free option)
50ml sunflower oil, plus extra for greasing
1 tsp vanilla extract

For the sauce
100g soft light brown sugar
2 tbsp cocoa powder

Equipment
You will need a 1.25 litre pudding bowl, 17cm in diameter at the top, for this recipe

Preheat the oven to 180°C (350°F), gas mark 4, and lightly grease the pudding bowl with sunflower oil.

Place the flaxseed in a small bowl and mix it with 6 tablespoons of water. Set aside to thicken while you prepare the other ingredients.

Sift the flour, baking powder and cocoa powder into a large mixing bowl, then whisk in the caster sugar and salt until evenly combined. Pour the rice milk, almond (or coconut) milk, sunflower oil and vanilla extract into a separate bowl and stir together.

Add the flaxseed mixture and milk mixture to the flour and whisk together into a rich, glossy batter. Pour the mixture into the prepared pudding bowl.

Next, prepare the ingredients for the sauce. In a separate bowl, combine the brown sugar and cocoa powder. Sprinkle the mixture over the top of the pudding and then carefully pour over 175ml of boiling water.

Place in the oven and bake for 55 minutes, during which time the pudding will rise up a little and become firm and slightly crunchy on top. Remove from the oven and serve from the bowl while hot.

baked
syrup sponge

Syrup sponge is one of those puddings that takes me straight back to my childhood; only ever made in the darkest and coldest of months (and even then, sparingly), it was a real treat and always came slathered in lashings of custard. Here, I've created a version that is both intolerance friendly and has all the luxurious sweetness of the original. Just the thing for a winter's evening – pour over some of my delicious vanilla custard (see page 213) and be transported back to your childhood or spark new food memories in your own children.

nut free   gluten free   vegan   soya free   yeast free

Serves 4

Grated zest and juice of
   1 lemon
5 tbsp golden syrup
100g dairy-free margarine,
   plus extra for greasing
100g golden caster sugar
2 heaped tsp egg replacer
   (ideally Orgran) whisked
   with 4 tbsp water
100g gluten-free self-raising
   flour (ideally Doves Farm)

Equipment
You will need a 1.25 litre
   pudding bowl, 17cm in
   diameter at the top, for
   this recipe

Preheat the oven to 180°C (350°F), gas mark 4, and lightly grease the pudding bowl with margarine.

Place the lemon zest and juice in the prepared pudding bowl, add the golden syrup and mix together.

Place the margarine and sugar in a large mixing bowl and cream together with a wooden spoon until combined. Stir in the egg replacer, a little at a time, then sift in the flour and mix in until just combined. Spoon the sponge mixture on top of the syrup and level the top with the back of a spoon.

Bake in the oven for 35 minutes or until firm to the touch and golden. Serve from the bowl while hot, spooning some of the sauce over each portion.

You can easily turn this pudding into a jam sponge by replacing the golden syrup with a jam of your choice – raspberry or blackberry work particularly well...

pumpkin pudding
with spiced toffee sauce

Think of a sticky toffee pudding but with an earthier, warmer note: less sugar and more spice. It is a fabulous way to use a squash or pumpkin and will imbue your kitchen with a sweet, spicy perfume that's impossible to resist. In my experience, children and adults love this pudding equally. Serve with a scoop of Vanilla or Chocolate Ice Cream (see pages 205 and 211) and prepare to feel indulged!

nut free   gluten free   vegan   soya free   yeast free

Serves 12

1 butternut squash
    (about 550g)
6 tbsp ground flaxseed
½ tsp gluten-free baking
    powder
200g soft light brown sugar
225ml sunflower oil, plus
    extra for greasing
225g gluten-free self-raising
    flour (ideally Doves Farm)
1 tsp bicarbonate of soda
2 tsp ground ginger
1 tsp ground cinnamon
½ tsp mixed spice

For the spiced toffee sauce
250ml rice or other dairy-
    free milk of your choice
100g soft light brown sugar
½ tsp mixed spice
1 tsp arrowroot

Equipment
You will need a 20cm square
    baking tin, about 7cm
    deep, for this recipe

Peel the squash, scooping out any seeds and pith, and cut into 2cm chunks. Bring a saucepan of water to the boil, add the squash and simmer for about 8 minutes or until the squash is completely cooked though and soft to the point of a knife. Drain in a colander and place in a food processor. Blitz into a smooth purée, then set aside to cool down.

Preheat the oven to 200°C (400°F), gas mark 6, then lightly grease the baking tin with sunflower oil and line with baking parchment.

Next, place the flaxseed and baking powder in a small bowl with 135ml of water and mix together until combined. Leave to sit and thicken while you prepare the other ingredients.

Place the sugar and sunflower oil in a large mixing bowl and whisk together vigorously for 2–3 minutes. Add the squash purée and flaxseed mixture to the sugar and oil and whisk together until combined. Sift in the flour, bicarbonate of soda and spices and then use a metal spoon to fold in the dry ingredients until fully incorporated.

Tip into the prepared tin and bake for 40–45 minutes or until risen and fragrant. Remove from the oven, leave to cool for a minute or two and then carefully lift out of the tin and set aside.

Meanwhile, make the sauce. Place the rice milk, sugar and mixed spice in a saucepan over a medium heat and gently cook until the sugar has dissolved and you have a smooth sauce. Bring to a simmer, then add the arrowroot and whisk into the sauce until it thickens and becomes nice and glossy. Cut the pudding into squares and serve with a generous pouring of the spiced toffee sauce.

glossary

In this section I've listed all the intolerance-friendly products that I've used in the recipes, together with websites of recommended suppliers for the more unusual items. You'll see I've also included a few basic recipes, such as for stock or apple purée, which you might like to make yourself rather than using a commercial product.

agar agar flakes

Made from dried seaweed, these provide a high-quality vegetarian alternative to gelatine and can be used in a variety of dairy-free and vegan recipes as a stabilising and thickening agent for custards, puddings and sauces. You can find it in health-food shops and certain supermarkets, as well as online:

www.ocado.co.uk
www.waitrose.co.uk

agave syrup

A naturally sweet syrup made from the juice obtained from the agave (tequila) plant. It is just as sweet as honey but not quite as sweet as golden syrup and can be used in place of either in your cooking and baking. Agave syrup also makes a good addition to homemade lemonade or cocktails, especially mojitos. You can buy it in health-food shops and most supermarkets.

raspberry fizz

gluten free, vegan, soya free, yeast free, nut free

Makes 1 litre

300g fresh raspberries
150ml agave syrup
1 litre sparkling water

Place the raspberries in a large bowl, pour over the syrup and muddle together using a spoon or fork. Leave to sit for 1 hour and then pass through a fine-mesh sieve into a large glass jug. Pour over the sparkling water and stir together. Serve on a hot day with ice.

almond extract

This extract has an intense marzipan flavour that makes it perfect for adding to all types of puddings. Don't get it confused with almond essence, which is a synthetic version with an overly sweet and chemical taste.

almond milk

A rich and creamy milk with a distinctive almond flavour, making it suitable for puddings and for pouring over granola and other cereals. You can make your own (see the recipe below) or buy it ready-made. Most varieties come sweetened with sugar or agave syrup, though you can find unsweetened options, which I prefer, notably the brands Blue Diamond and Alpro. I recommend the following:

Alpro
www.goodnessdirect.co.uk
www.morrisons.co.uk
www.ocado.co.uk
www.sainsburys.co.uk
www.waitrose.co.uk
Blue Diamond
www.sainsburys.co.uk
www.waitrose.co.uk
Ecomil
www.goodnessdirect.co.uk
Provamel
www.goodnessdirect.co.uk

almond milk `contains nuts`

gluten free, vegan, soya free, yeast free

Makes 1 litre
200g blanched almonds
1–2 tbsp runny honey or maple syrup

Soak the almonds in water for 6–24 hours (the longer the better). Drain the nuts and place in a blender with 1 litre of water, then blitz until you have a creamy white liquid with as few bits in it as possible. Pour the contents through a nut-milk bag (available online at www.goodnessdirect.co.uk) or fine piece of muslin. Squeeze the bag gently until all of the liquid has filtered through and you have only almond pulp in the bag/ muslin. Stir in the honey or maple syrup, the amount depending on how sweet you like the milk, then decant into a clean bottle or jar and refrigerate until ready to use. Stored like this, it will keep for up to four days. You will have to shake the milk before use as it can separate.

apple purée

Apples simply cooked and puréed can be used as an egg replacer when making cakes, biscuits or muffins. To replace one egg in a recipe, use 2 rounded tablespoons of apple purée and ½ teaspoon of baking powder, adding the baking powder to the dry ingredients and the apple purée to the fat. You can buy it ready-made or you can make your own (see recipe below). I can also recommend the following brands:
  *Biona
    www.goodnessdirect.co.uk
  *Clearspring
    www.goodnessdirect.co.uk
    www.waitrose.co.uk

apple purée

gluten free, vegan, soya free, yeast free, nut free

Makes 200g
2 Bramley apples
2 tbsp apple juice or water

Peel and core the apples, chop into small cubes and combine in a saucepan with the apple juice or water. Cook over a low heat, stirring occasionally, for around 10 minutes, or until stewed and softened, then blitz in a food processor into a smooth purée. Pour into a sterilised jar and store in the fridge, where it will keep for up to five days.

arrowroot

A natural plant-based starch, arrowroot can be used to thicken sauces, custards, puddings and drinks (see also cornflour). It is often favoured in sweet cooking as, unlike other starches, arrowroot does not make sauces go cloudy but leaves them smooth and clear.

baking powder

This is a leavening agent, used to give volume to and lighten the texture of your baking (see also bicarbonate of soda). There are a number of reliable gluten-free brands. I recommend the following:
  *Doves Farm
    www.dovesfarm.co.uk
    www.goodnessdirect.co.uk
    www.sainsburys.co.uk
  *Dr Oetker
    www.goodnessdirect.co.uk
    www.sainsburys.co.uk

basmati rice

Native to India and Pakistan, basmati is a long-grained variety of rice, subtle in flavour and sweetly fragrant. It is available as white (polished) or brown (wholegrain), the latter being higher in fibre. Wonderful in a wide range of rice-based dishes and especially as an

glossary

accompaniment to curries or grilled meats and fish, basmati is also a good choice for delicate salads and stuffings. It can be cooked in stock or water.

bicarbonate of soda

Bicarbonate of soda, sometimes referred to as 'baking soda', is used in cooking as a leavening agent (see also baking powder). It reacts with the liquid in batters, creating a characteristically light texture and grain in pancakes, cakes, soda bread and other baked foods. The reaction does not occur until the mixture is heated, however, meaning that you can leave your cake mixture or other type of batter to stand at room temperature without rising until it is heated in the oven.

camargue red rice

A short-grained variety of rice from the Camargue region of southern France, brownish red in colour and with a nutty taste and bite. Perfect for making into hearty salads or serving as an accompaniment to grilled fish or chicken. Best cooked using stock.

chinese five-spice powder

A fragrant blend of ground cinnamon, Sichuan pepper, star anise, cloves and fennel seeds, this goes well with chicken, pork and fish and is integral to any stir-fry or Chinese-style marinade.

stir-fry marinade for chicken

`nut-free option`

gluten free, vegan, soya free, yeast free, nut-free option

Serves 4

1 heaped tsp gluten- and yeast-free stock powder
1–2 cloves of garlic
2.5cm piece of root ginger
1 tbsp toasted sesame oil (or smoked rapeseed oil for a nut-free option)
1 tbsp lemon juice
1 tbsp soft light brown sugar
1 tsp Chinese five-spice powder

Combine the stock powder and 100ml of boiling water until dissolved. Grate in the garlic and ginger, mix in the other ingredients and then use as a marinade for chicken or fish, or add to vegetables or rice noodles while you're stir-frying them.

chorizo

A dense, spicy, coarse-textured pork sausage from Spain, seasoned with black pepper, paprika and chillies. You can find it in most supermarkets and delis, either ready-cooked or fresh, but be sure to check the ingredients as many varieties contain milk proteins. A high-quality brand to look for is:

*Foods Unearthed
www.ocado.co.uk
www.waitrose.co.uk

chocolate & cocoa powder

Both dark chocolate and cocoa powder are suitable for use in intolerance-friendly baking. Look for a high-quality variety with a high percentage of cocoa solids (a minimum of 70 per cent, ideally) that is both dairy and soya free. I recommend the following brands:

*Green & Black's (for cocoa powder)
www.goodnessdirect.co.uk
www.ocado.co.uk
www.sainsburys.co.uk

www.waitrose.co.uk
Montezuma's
www.goodnessdirect.co.uk
www.ocado.co.uk
www.waitrose.co.uk
Willie's Cacao
www.ocado.co.uk
www.waitrose.co.uk

luxury dark hot chocolate `nut-free option`

gluten free, vegan, soya free, yeast free, nut-free option

Serves 4

100g dairy- and soya-free dark chocolate, broken into pieces, plus extra for grating
4 tbsp agave or maple syrup
750ml almond milk (or rice milk for a nut-free option)

Melt the chocolate and the syrup in a bowl set in a saucepan of gently simmering water. Heat the almond (or rice) milk in a separate pan until hot but not simmering. Pour into the melted chocolate, bit by bit and stirring as you go, until you have a smooth, rich hot chocolate. Serve in mugs with a little extra chocolate grated on top.

coconut cream

This is obtained by chilling and separating coconut milk, then scooping off the condensed section from the remaining water to make the cream. Perfect for using in curries, soups and sauces, it can also be whisked with icing sugar for a delicious 'whipped cream'. Coconut cream is available in small cartons and tins from most supermarkets.

coconut milk

A rich and creamy sweet white milk made by soaking fresh or desiccated coconut in warm water and then squeezing it through a nut-milk bag (obtainable online from www.goodness-direct.co.uk) or fine muslin cloth. Suitable for adding to curry dishes and puddings, it's available in tinned form from most supermarkets. You can also buy a much thinner version of coconut milk – much as you can with rice milk or almond milk – that comes in a carton and is better for pouring over cereal, for instance, or using in a drink. I recommend this version of coconut milk for making my Coconut and Mango Smoothie (see page 19).

coconut oil

Coconut oil is an edible oil extracted from the 'meat' of ripe coconuts. Solid at room temperature, it turns to liquid when warmed. Famed for its health benefits, it works brilliantly in place of butter or oil in baking recipes and in curries, though it does lend a distinctive coconut flavour to whatever dish you are making. For online suppliers, see:
www.goodnessdirect.co.uk
www.ocado.co.uk

coconut yoghurt

Made from the pulp of fresh coconuts and a naturally derived dairy-free probiotic, coconut yoghurt has a thick and creamy texture, making it perfect as a topping for granola (see page 21) or for serving with fresh fruit, drizzled with honey. Alternatively, serve with cakes and puddings in lieu of cream. I recommend the following brand:
Coyo Coconut Yoghurt
www.goodnessdirect.co.uk

cornflour

Cornflour is a natural starch derived from maize. Useful in cooking to thicken sauces, custard, ice cream, soups and gravy. If you can't tolerate cornflour, arrowroot often makes a good substitute.

custard powder

If you don't want to make your own custard (see page 213), then you can cheat and use custard powder. Mix with a dairy-free milk of your choice to make a rich custard, or use in its powdered form to add to biscuits or cakes for a light texture and vanilla flavour.

All Natural Custard Powder
www.goodnessdirect.co.uk
www.waitrose.co.uk

Bird's Custard Powder
www.morrisons.co.uk
www.ocado.co.uk
www.sainsburys.co.uk
www.waitrose.co.uk

egg replacer

Consisting of natural starches and gums, a commercial egg replacer is a good substitute for eggs in cakes, breads and biscuits. I recommend Orgran, available from health-food shops and online:
www.goodnessdirect.co.uk
(See also apple purée, ground flaxseed.)

flour

Doves Farm specialises in blending their own range of gluten-free flours and I cannot recommend them highly enough. Made from a combination of rice flour, tapioca, buckwheat and potato flour, they are the perfect all-rounders for pastry, biscuits, cakes and breads. They are also widely available from most supermarkets, as well as online:
www.dovesfarm.co.uk
www.goodnessdirect.co.uk
www.morrisons.co.uk
www.ocado.co.uk
www.sainsburys.co.uk
www.waitrose.co.uk
(For other types of gluten-free flour, see gram flour, rice flour.)

garlic oil

A natural olive oil infused with garlic, it's a pleasing and slightly lazy way of getting garlic into your cooking. Perfect for using as part of a dressing or for drizzling over roasted vegetables.

gram flour

A dense, golden flour made from ground chickpeas, gram flour has a wonderfully mellow flavour and is brilliant for using as a coating or for making into breads (see Roasted Vegetable Socca on page 71). Available from most supermarkets, as well as online:
www.dovesfarm.co.uk
www.goodnessdirect.co.uk
www.morrisons.co.uk
www.ocado.co.uk
www.sainsburys.co.uk
www.waitrose.co.uk

ground flaxseed

Also known as ground linseed, ground flaxseed is a good egg replacer in cakes and biscuits, its malty flavour making it more suitable for inclusion in rich baked items, such as chocolate cake or banana bread. To replace one egg, use 2 tablespoons of ground flaxseed mixed together with 3 tablespoons of water and leave to sit for 5 minutes to thicken up. Ground flaxseed is available from some supermarkets and all health-food shops. I recommend the following brands:

Linwoods
www.goodnessdirect.co.uk
www.sainsburys.co.uk

Prewetts Ground Flaxseed
www.goodnessdirect.co.uk

ground rice

Not to be confused with rice flour, this consists of coarsely ground grains of rice. Traditionally used in baking and for puddings, it adds lightness and texture to cakes and tarts. You will find it in health-food shops and most supermarkets, in the rice and grains section, rather than with the flour. If you can't get ground rice, ground almonds are a good substitute.

groundnut oil

This is a clear, pinkish-golden liquid made by pressing specially grown peanuts from Spain, China and India. The refined variety has a better pouring consistency than non-refined peanut oil, and its bland flavour makes it ideal for cooking. It has a high heat resistance, too, so does not burn easily.

maple syrup

A sweetener made from the sap of the maple tree, usually from Canada. Be sure to check it is pure maple syrup rather than anything synthetic. Perfect for pouring over pancakes or ice cream and for using in smoothies.

margarine

There are a number of dairy-free margarines on the market, all varying in cookability and flavour. It's a good idea to check the ingredients carefully, though, and to buy only the trans-fat-free varieties. I can recommend the following:

Biona Sunflower Margarine
www.goodnessdirect.co.uk
Pure Sunflower Spread
www.goodnessdirect.co.uk
www.ocado.co.uk
www.sainsburys.co.uk
www.waitrose.co.uk

mustard

Made from finely ground mustard seeds, mustard powder is useful both as a condiment and as part of a marinade or baste. For 1 tablespoon of English mustard, mix together 1 heaped tablespoon of mustard powder and 1 tablespoon of water. I recommend Colman's

Mustard Powder for a basic store-cupboard staple, or you can make your own mustard:

---

wholegrain mustard

gluten free, vegan, soya free, yeast free, nut free

Makes 250g

2 cloves of garlic
175g brown mustard seeds
½ tsp ground ginger
1 tsp ground cinnamon
½ tsp freshly grated nutmeg
15 peppercorns, coarsely ground
¼ tsp dried thyme
2 tsp dried chervil
2 tsp dried tarragon
3 bay leaves
1 tsp sea salt flakes
300ml unsweetened grape juice

Finely chop the garlic and place in a bowl with the mustard seeds, spices, herbs and salt, then pour over the grape juice, cover with a plate or cling film and leave to soak for 24–48 hours, topping up with a little extra liquid if necessary – the seeds should be just covered. Scoop out the bay leaves, place the mixture in a food processor and blitz until fine. Push through a fine-mesh sieve and then spoon into small sterilised jars and store, out of direct light, for at least two weeks before using.

---

nori

Thin sheets of dried, vitamin-packed seaweed used in Japanese-style dishes and for making sushi. Available from supermarkets and specialist shops, as well as online:

www.goodnessdirect.co.uk
www.ocado.co.uk
www.sainsburys.co.uk
www.waitrose.co.uk

pasta

Gluten-free pasta and spaghetti tends to be made with either maize or rice flour. You can buy a number of decent varieties. I recommend the following brands:

Doves Farm
www.dovesfarm.co.uk
www.morrisons.co.uk
www.ocado.co.uk
www.sainsburys.co.uk
www.waitrose.co.uk

Orgran (for macaroni)
www.goodnessdirect.co.uk

Salute
www.ocado.co.uk
www.waitrose.co.uk

pine nuts

Probably best known for their use in pesto sauce, pine nuts have a very delicate taste and texture and are high in protein, which makes them especially valuable in a vegetarian diet. Eaten raw, they have a soft texture and a sweet, buttery flavour that goes especially well in salads. They are delicious toasted, as this brings out their flavour and adds a little extra crunch. They can also be soaked and then blitzed to make a very convincing 'cream sauce' for pasta.

pesto

`contains nuts`

gluten free, vegan, soya free, yeast free,

Makes 150g
100g pine nuts
A large bunch of basil
3 tbsp extra-virgin olive oil
Sea salt flakes and freshly ground black pepper

Preheat the oven to 200°C (400°F), gas mark 6. Toast the pine nuts on a baking tray in the oven, shaking the tray occasionally to ensure they don't burn, for 5–6 minutes or until they are golden. Place the toasted pine nuts in a food processor with the remaining ingredients and a pinch of salt and blitz into a smooth purée. Season with pepper and extra salt to taste and add a little more olive oil if you think it's necessary. Store in a clean jar in the fridge for up to four days.

polenta

Used extensively in Italy, polenta is finely ground cornmeal that is traditionally made into a creamy paste or left to cool and set, and then fried, grilled or baked to make a crisp, dense addition to roasted meat or vegetables. You can also use it in its ground form instead of breadcrumbs to coat chicken or fish before frying to create a crisp and golden crumb.

porridge oats

The vast majority of oats and oat products on the market are contaminated with wheat, rye and/or barley during both cultivation and processing, making them unsuitable for people avoiding gluten. The gluten-free variety is grown and processed separately from any other grain crops, making it safe for gluten-free diets. Available in all health-food shops and online: www.goodnessdirect.co.uk

preserved lemons

Lemons are rubbed with salt, packed in jars and covered with lemon juice and then left for about four weeks. The result is intensely flavoured moist fruit perfect for Ottoman-style cooking. Remove the flesh, rinse and slice the rind to add to salads, marinades and stews. You can buy preserved lemons in certain supermarkets, delis and health-food shops, or you can make your own:

preserved lemons

gluten free, vegan, soya free, yeast free, nut free

Makes 1 x 1kg Kilner jar

12 lemons
250g sea salt flakes

Cut 6 of the lemons into quarters, leaving them joined at the base by about 1cm. Juice the remaining 6 lemons. Pack 1 tablespoon of salt into each lemon and squash the quarters back into shape. Wedge them into the Kilner jar, having first sterilised it. Pour over the lemon juice (if there's not enough liquid to fill the jar, top with extra lemon juice), then seal the jar. Rotate the jar every few days, turning it upside down to get the liquid moving and hence to redistribute the salt, and leave for 4–6 weeks.

puy lentils

Hailing from France, these dark, dense, mottled lentils have a distinctive earthy flavour and incomparable nutty texture. I eat them most often in salads or simply dressed as a side dish for fish, poultry or game. If you have any leftover meat – roast lamb, beef, pork or chicken – chop it into cubes and toss with dressed Puy lentils and a handful of flat-leaf parsley, rocket or other peppery leaves.

quinoa

Actually a fruit rather than a grain (and pronounced 'keen-wah'), it can be used in much the same way as rice or couscous; that is to say, it makes a great accompaniment to grilled meats, fish or tagines or an addition to a salad. It has a slightly nutty texture but barely any flavour, hence I'd recommend cooking it in stock to enhance the taste.

rapeseed oil

When cold-pressed, rapeseed provides a cooking oil with a grassy, 'green' taste. It is suitable for baking and frying as well as dressing and dips, and is a good staple oil to have in your store cupboard. Meanwhile, smoked rapeseed oil makes a good alternative, taste-wise, to smoked sesame oil.

rice flour

Naturally gluten free and created from finely ground grains of rice, rice flour is traditionally used to make rice noodles. It can be used to thicken soups and stews and works very successfully in gluten-free baking. (See also ground rice.)

rice milk

A light and creamy milk with a naturally sweet taste made from soaked and very finely ground rice. I recommend the following brands:
  Alpro
  www.goodnessdirect.co.uk
  www.sainsburys.co.uk
  Provamel
  www.goodnessdirect.co.uk

sausages

You can now buy a range of gluten-free sausages from supermarkets and butchers. Check ingredients carefully for inclusion of eggs or soya. I recommend:
  Musk's Gluten-free Sausages
  www.ocado.co.uk
  www.sainsburys.co.uk
  www.waitrose.co.uk

glossary

stock

Flavoured, strained liquid made from the slow simmering of vegetables, herbs and bones. You can buy gluten-, dairy- and yeast-free stock powders and fresh stock from health-food shops and some supermarkets, or you can make your own (see recipes below). I recommend the following brands:

*Kallo
www.goodnessdirect.co.uk
www.waitrose.co.uk

*Marigold Swill Bouillon
www.goodnessdirect.co.uk
www.ocado.co.uk
www.waitrose.co.uk

chicken stock

*gluten free, dairy free,
egg free, soya free, yeast free, nut free*

Makes 1.5–2 litres

2 sticks of celery
1 carrot
1 onion
2 cloves of garlic
4 bay leaves
1 tsp freshly ground black pepper
1 x 1.5kg chicken (or chicken carcass)

Roughly chop the vegetables, then place with all the remaining ingredients in a large saucepan or casserole dish and add 2.5 litres of water. Bring to the boil and then reduce to a very low simmer. Cover with a lid and cook for 1 hour, checking from time to time and spooning off any foam that collects on the top of the water, until the chicken (if using) is cooked through and tender. Remove the chicken (or carcass) and strain the stock, discarding the vegetables. Decant the stock into one or more airtight containers and store in the fridge for up to three days or in the freezer for up to three months. Cut up the cooked chicken to use in salads, sandwiches or pasta.

vegetable stock

gluten free, vegan, soya free, yeast free, nut free

Makes 1.5–2 litres

2 onions
1 clove of garlic
1 heart of celery
1 parsnip
1 small butternut squash
2 carrots
2 bay leaves
A small bunch of mixed herbs (such as marjoram, tarragon, parsley and/or oregano)
1 tsp freshly ground black pepper

Roughly chop the vegetables, then place with all the remaining ingredients in a large saucepan or casserole dish and add 2.5 litres of water. Bring to the boil and then reduce to a very low simmer. Cover with a lid and cook for 2 hours, checking from time to time and spooning off any foam that collects on the top of the water. Strain the stock, discarding the vegetables, and decant into one or more airtight containers. It can be stored in the fridge for up to three days or in the freezer for up to three months.

sunflower oil

A good all-round, neutral-tasting oil suitable for baking and frying.

sunflower seed butter

Rich and nutty, sunflower seed butter is not dissimilar to peanut butter but has a slightly more savoury taste. Use instead of tahini for a nut-free option. You can make your own (see recipe below) or buy it in jars in health-food shops and online:

www.goodnessdirect.co.uk

sunflower seed butter

gluten free, vegan, soya free, yeast free, nut free

Makes about 60g

4 heaped tbsp sunflower seeds
1 tbsp extra-virgin olive oil
1 tbsp maple syrup
A small pinch of sea salt flakes

In a heavy-based frying pan, dry-fry the sunflower seeds over a medium-high heat, shaking the pan regularly to ensure they don't burn, for 4–5 minutes or until lightly browned and then blitz in a food processor with the remaining ingredients until just smooth. Store in a sealed tub or jar in the fridge for up to one week.

tahini

Made from ground, hulled sesame seeds, this rich, nutty paste can be served on its own as a dip or used as the base for hummus and other dishes, including halva and some sweet puddings. You can find it in most supermarkets. If you can't eat sesame seeds, then sunflower seed butter makes a good alternative.

tamarind paste

A paste made from the fruit (separated from the pod and seeds) of the tamarind tree, it has an intense, sweet-sharp flavour that makes it ideal for using in marinades and sauces. Available from most supermarkets and health-food shops.

toasted sesame oil

Made from toasted sesame seeds, this dark and pungent oil adds a smoky quality to dressings and marinades. Smoked rapeseed oil makes a good nut-free alternative.

vanilla bean paste

Used in ice cream, custard and other sweet sauces, this syrupy paste adds a distinctive flavour and appearance due to the flecks of seeds from the vanilla pod. Available from most supermarkets.

vanilla extract

Proper vanilla extract is made by macerating vanilla pods – not to be confused with vanilla essence, which is a synthetic, chemically based version of the real thing. Rich and pure, vanilla extract can be used in ice cream, custard, baking and drinks.

vegetable shortening

The inclusion of shortening is really the only way to ensure crisp and 'short' pastry made from gluten- and dairy-free ingredients. Essentially a vegetable version of lard, it can be found in the chilled aisle next to the margarine in most supermarkets; I recommend using Trex Vegetable Shortening.

xanthan gum

A plant gum that acts like the gluten present in wheat, it helps pull your baking together, allowing you to make pastry that can be rolled out and adding a good crumb to cakes and bread. It can be found in certain supermarkets, as well as health-food shops and online:
www.dovesfarm.co.uk
www.goodnessdirect.co.uk
www.sainsburys.co.uk
www.waitrose.co.uk

breads, scones & muffins

Butter Bean & Parsnip Scones 86
Butternut Squash & Tomato Muffins 91
Chickpea Bread for Toast & Jam 28
Chickpea Pancakes 172
Chocolate Malted Muffins 98
Cornbread 156
Focaccia 180
Maple Syrup Scones 27
Peanut Butter & Banana Muffins 22
Pizza Bread 124
Potato Farls 26
Roasted Vegetable Socca 71
Spiced Onion Muffins 81
Sweet Potato Bread 78

soups

Butternut Squash, Lentil, Honey & Thyme Soup 178
King Prawn Gazpacho 54
Parsnip, Chilli & Lemon Soup 89
Pea Soup with Crispy Chorizo Croutons 176
Tomato & Almond Soup 185

salads

Carrot & Orange Salad 68
Chicken, Fennel & Raisin Red Rice Salad 74
Chicken, Roasted Tomato & Caper Herb Salad 69
Chicory, Ham, Sweet Potato & Sun-dried Tomato Salad 88
Quinoa Tabbouleh 66
Spiced Squash, Avocado & Mixed Sprout Salad 80
Watercress & Radish Salad with Avocado Dressing 53

meat

Baked Italian Chicken & Rice 140
Baked Leg of Lamb with Lemon, Garlic & Oregano 179
Bang Bang Chicken 130
Busy Boston Baked Beans 118
Chestnut & Chorizo Stew 168

Chicken & Preserved Lemon Tagine 165
Chicken, Artichoke & Caper Stew 149
Chicken Ballotine with Courgette & Herb Cheese Stuffing 59–60
Chicken Nuggets with Barbecue Sauce 116
Chicken Schnitzel with Salsa Verde 52
Chicken with Caraway, Olives & Orange 188
Chilli con Carne
Creamy Chicken Curry 141
Creamy Garlic, Herb & Crispy Bacon Stuffed Potatoes 127
Grilled Chermoula Chicken with Avocado Quinoa Salad 67
Herb-Crusted Rack of Lamb with Sloe Gin Gravy & Butter Bean Mash 197–8
Lamb, Apricot & Tahini Meatballs 171
Lamb Burgers with Beetroot Hummus 192
Lemon & Ginger Chicken 190
Lemon & Oregano Lamb Kebabs 64
Marmalade-Baked Chicken 134
Masala Chicken 159
Poached Chicken with Walnut Sauce 186–7
Rolled Breast of Chicken with Artichoke Purée 82–3
Roast Pork with Potatoes, Lemon, Fennel & Capers 144
Sausage, Lentil & Sun-dried Tomato Cassoulet 158
Seared Chicken Breasts with Spiced Coconut Rice 137
Shepherd's Pie 127
Sweet and Sour Chicken 189
Whole Roast Jerk Chicken 147–8

fish

Fish Pie 128
Grilled Tiger Prawns with Avocado Cream 182
Hot-Smoked Salmon Kedgeree with Cashew Sauce 29

Salmon & Avocado Sushi Bowls with Ginger & Sesame Dressing 85
Salmon, New Potato & Pea Salad with Mint Pesto Dressing 76–7
Sweet Chilli & Sesame Salmon 150

vegetarian

Baby Squash with Leeks & Garlic & Herb Cheese 164
Butter Bean Hummus with Mint Oil 173
Caramelised Onion Tart 61–2
Creamy Caponata Bake 166–7
Dhal with Caraway Aubergine 160
Garlic & Herb Cashew Cream Cheese 55
Moroccan Vegetable Tagine 142
Patatas Bravas 184
Piquant Potato Wedges 119
Roasted Tomato & Basil Sauce 120
Spicy Bean Burgers with Avocado Salsa 194–5
Stir-fry Jasmine Rice 191
Sweet Potato & Onion Bhaji Bites 162

pasta

Creamy Chicken, Herb & Mushroom Penne 136
Macaroni Cheese 121
Peperonata, Pea & Olive Pasta 57
Prawn & Chorizo Spaghetti 138
Spaghetti & Meatballs 122

puddings & sweet dishes

Apple & Blackberry Pie 206–7
Apple Pancakes with Cinnamon Roasted Fruit 24
Baked Syrup Sponge 221
Banana, Maple & Oat Smoothie 18
Chocolate & Coconut Crunch 212
Chocolate Ice Cream 211
Coconut & Mango Smoothie 19
Decadent Chocolate Tart 214
French Apple Tart 216–18

Gooey Chocolate Pudding 220
Gooseberry & Redcurrant Woodland Crumble with Vanilla Custard 213
Granola with Banana 'Yoghurt' 21
Lemon & Coconut Tartlets 101
Lemon Curd 97
Lemon Tart 202–4
Mango & Pineapple Puddings 208
Pumpkin Pudding with Spiced Toffee Sauce 222
Rhubarb & Ginger Sponge 219
Strawberry Ice Cream 210
Vanilla Ice Cream 205

cakes & biscuits

Brown Sugar Oat Biscuits 34
Carrot & Ginger Squares with Lemon Icing
Cherry & Almond Biscuits 39
Chocolate Banana Bread 46
Chocolate Celebration Cake 110–12
Chocolate Chip Biscuits 33
Christmas Biscuits 44
Coconut Loaf 45
Gingerbread Loaf 106
Honey & Blueberry Drizzle Cake 96
Lemon Butterfly Cakes 113
Lemon Loaf Cake 36
Lemon Shortbread 41
Mississippi Mud Brownies 43
Oat & Stem Ginger Cookies 38
Parsnip & Apple Cake with Orange Icing 94
Rhubarb & Apple Traybake 102
Spiced Apple Cake 108
Spicy Cinnamon Cookies 42
St Clement's Cake 105
Strawberry & Cream Cupcakes 48
Sunflower Seed Butter Cookies 32
Vanilla Bundt Cake 109

index

a

agar flakes 224
agave syrup 224
almonds
    almond extract 224
    almond milk 224–5
    cherry & almond biscuits 39
apples
    apple & blackberry pie 206–7
    apple pancakes with cinnamon-roasted fruit 24
    apple purée 225
    French apple tart 216–18
    parsnip & apple cake with orange icing 94
    rhubarb & apple traybake 102
    spiced apple cake 108
    vanilla bundt cake 109
apricots
    lamb, apricot and tahini meatballs 171
arrowroot 225
artichokes
    chicken, artichoke & caper stew 149
    rolled breast of chicken with artichoke purée 82–3
aubergines
    creamy caponata bake 166–7
    dhal with caraway aubergine 160
avocados
    avocado dressing 53
    grilled chermoula chicken with avocado quinoa salad 67
    grilled tiger prawns with avocado cream 182
    salmon & avocado sushi bowls 85
    spiced squash, avocado & mixed sprout salad 80
    spicy bean burgers with avocado salsa 194–6

b

bacon
    baked Italian chicken & rice 140
    creamy garlic, herb & crispy bacon stuffed potatoes 126
baked syrup sponge 221
baking powder 225
bananas
    banana, maple & oat smoothie 18
    banana 'yoghurt' 21
    chocolate banana bread 46
    peanut butter & banana muffins 22
bang bang chicken 130
barbecue sauce 116
beans
    busy Boston baked beans 118
    butter bean hummus with mint oil 173
    chilli con carne 154
    spicy bean burgers with avocado salsa 194–6
beef
    chilli con carne 154
    spaghetti & meatballs 122
beetroot hummus 192
bhaji bites, sweet potato & onion 162
bicarbonate of soda 226
biscuits 14–15
    brown sugar oat biscuits 34
    cherry & almond biscuits 39
    chocolate chip biscuits 33
    Christmas biscuits 44
    lemon shortbread 41
    oat & stem ginger cookies 38
    spicy cinnamon cookies 42
    sunflower seed butter cookies 32
blackberries
    apple & blackberry pie 206–7
blueberries
    honey & blueberry drizzle cake 96
Boston baked beans 118
bread
    chickpea bread 28
    cornbread 156

focaccia 180
roasted vegetable socca 71
sweet potato bread 78
brown sugar oat biscuits 34
brownies, Mississippi mud 43
burgers
    lamb burgers with beetroot hummus 192
    spicy bean burgers with avocado salsa 194–6
butter beans
    butter bean & parsnip scones 86
    butter bean hummus with mint oil 173
    butter bean mash 197–8
butternut squash see squash

c

cakes
    carrot & ginger squares with lemon icing 104
    chocolate banana bread 46
    chocolate celebration cake 110–12
    coconut loaf 45
    gingerbread loaf 106
    honey & blueberry drizzle cake 96
    lemon butterfly cakes 113
    lemon loaf cake 36
    Mississippi mud brownies 43
    parsnip & apple cake with orange icing 94
    rhubarb & apple traybake 102
    St Clement's cake 105
    spiced apple cake 108
    strawberry & cream cupcakes 48
    vanilla bundt cake 109
caponata bake 166–7
caramelised onion tart 61–2
carrots
    carrot & ginger squares with lemon icing 104
    carrot & orange salad 68
cashew nuts
    cashew sauce 29
    cream sauce 166–7

garlic & herb cashew cream cheese 55
cassoulet, sausage, lentil & sun-dried tomato 158
chermoula chicken with avocado quinoa salad 67
cherry & almond biscuits 39
chestnut & chorizo stew 168
chicken
    baked Italian chicken & rice 140
    bang bang chicken 130
    chicken & preserved lemon tagine 165
    chicken, artichoke & caper stew 149
    chicken ballotine with courgette & herb cheese stuffing 59–60
    chicken, fennel & raisin red rice salad 74
    chicken nuggets with barbecue sauce 116
    chicken, roasted tomato & caper herb salad 69
    chicken schnitzel with salsa verde 52
    chicken with caraway, olives & orange 188
    creamy chicken curry 141
    creamy chicken, herb & mushroom penne 136
    grilled chermoula chicken with avocado quinoa salad 67
    lemon & ginger chicken 190
    marmalade-baked chicken 134
    masala chicken 159
    poached chicken with walnut sauce 186–7
    rolled breast of chicken with artichoke purée 82–3
    seared chicken breasts with spiced coconut rice 137
    stir-fry marinade for chicken 226
    stock 232
    sweet & sour chicken 189
    whole roast jerk chicken 147–8
chickpeas

chickpea bread 28
chickpea pancakes 172
sweet potato & onion bhaji
bites 162
chicory, ham, sweet potato
& sun-dried tomato
salad 88
chilli
chilli con carne 154
parsnip, chilli & lemon
soup 89
sweet chilli & sesame
salmon 150
Chinese five-spice powder
226
chocolate 226–7
chocolate & coconut
crunch 212
chocolate banana bread
46
chocolate celebration
cake 110–12
chocolate chip biscuits 33
chocolate ice cream 211
chocolate malted muffins
98
decadent chocolate tart
214
gooey chocolate pudding
220
luxury dark hot chocolate
227
Mississippi mud brownies
43
chorizo 226
chestnut & chorizo stew
168
pea soup with crispy
chorizo croutons 176
prawn & chorizo spaghetti
138
Christmas biscuits 44
cinnamon cookies 42
cocoa powder 226–7
coconut
coconut loaf 45
lemon & coconut tartlets
101
coconut cream 227
coconut milk 227
coconut & mango
smoothie 19
creamy chicken curry 141
parsnip, chilli & lemon
soup 89

seared chicken breasts
with spiced coconut
rice 137
coconut oil 227
chocolate & coconut
crunch 212
coconut yoghurt 227
cod
fish pie 128
cookies 14–15
oat & stem ginger cookies
38
spicy cinnamon cookies
42
sunflower seed butter
cookies 32
cornbread 156
cornflour 227
courgettes
chicken ballotine
with courgette & herb
cheese stuffing
59–60
creamy caponata bake 166–7
crumble, gooseberry &
redcurrant woodland 213
cupcakes, strawberry &
cream 48
curry
creamy chicken curry 141
masala chicken 159
custard 228
vanilla custard 213

d
dates
decadent chocolate tart
214
Mississippi mud brownies
43
dhal with caraway aubergine
160
dill & mustard dressing 76
dried fruit
granola with banana
'yoghurt' 21

e
egg replacer 228

f
farls, potato 26
fennel

chicken, fennel & raisin
red rice salad 74
roast pork with potatoes,
lemon, fennel &
capers 144
fish 15
fish pie 128
see also cod, salmon etc
flaxseed, ground 228
flour 228
focaccia 180
French apple tart 216–18
fruit: cinnamon-roasted fruit
24
see also apples,
strawberries etc

g
garlic & herb cashew cream
cheese 55
garlic oil 228
gazpacho, king prawn 54
ginger
carrot & ginger squares
with lemon icing 104
gingerbread loaf 106
oat & stem ginger cookies
38
rhubarb & ginger sponge
219
gooseberry & redcurrant
woodland crumble 213
gram flour 228
granola with banana
'yoghurt' 21
groundnut oil 229

h
ham
chicory, ham, sweet
potato & sun-dried
tomato salad 88
herbs 15
honey & blueberry drizzle
cake 96
hummus
beetroot hummus 192
butter bean hummus 173

i
ice cream
chocolate ice cream 211
strawberry ice cream 210
vanilla ice cream 205

k
kebabs, lemon & oregano
lamb 64
kedgeree, hot-smoked
salmon 29
kidney beans
chilli con carne 154
spicy bean burgers with
avocado salsa 194–6

l
lamb
baked leg of lamb with
lemon, garlic &
oregano 179
herb-crusted rack of lamb
with sloe gin & butter
bean mash 197–8
lamb, apricot and tahini
meatballs 171
lamb burgers with
beetroot hummus 192
lemon & oregano lamb
kebabs 64
shepherd's pie 127
leeks
baby squash with leeks &
garlic & herb cheese
164
lemon
carrot & ginger squares
with lemon icing 104
lemon & coconut tartlets
101
lemon & ginger chicken
190
lemon & oregano lamb
kebabs 64
lemon butterfly cakes 113
lemon curd 97
lemon loaf cake 36
lemon shortbread 41
lemon tart 202–4
preserved lemons 231
St Clement's cake 105
lentils 231
butternut squash, lentil,
honey & thyme
soup 178
dhal with caraway
aubergine 160
sausage, lentil & sun-dried
tomato cassoulet 158

m

macaroni cheese 121
mangoes
  coconut & mango
    smoothie 19
  mango & pineapple
    puddings 208
maple syrup 229
  maple syrup scones 27
margarine 14, 229
marmalade
  marmalade-baked
    chicken 134
  St Clement's cake 105
masala chicken 159
meat 15
  see also beef, lamb etc
meatballs
  lamb, apricot and tahini
    meatballs 171
  spaghetti & meatballs 122
mint pesto dressing 76
Mississippi mud brownies 43
Moroccan vegetable tagine
  142
muffins
  butternut squash & tomato
    muffins 91
  chocolate malted muffins
    98
  peanut butter & banana
    muffins 22
  spiced onion muffins 81
mushrooms
  creamy chicken, herb &
    mushroom penne 136
mustard 229

n

nori 229
nuts, toasting 14

o

oats 230
  brown sugar oat biscuits
    34
  granola with banana
    'yoghurt' 21
  oat & stem ginger cookies
    38
oils 14
olives
  peperonata, pea & olive
    pasta 57

onions
  caramelised onion tart
    61–2
  spiced onion muffins 81
  sweet potato & onion bhaji
    bites 162
  whole roast jerk chicken
    147–8
oranges
  carrot & orange salad 68
  parsnip & apple cake with
    orange icing 94
ovens 15

p

pancakes
  apple pancakes with
    cinnamon-roasted
    fruit 24
  chickpea pancakes 172
parsnips
  butter bean & parsnip
    scones 86
  parsnip & apple cake with
    orange icing 94
  parsnip, chilli & lemon
    soup 89
pasta 230
  creamy chicken, herb &
    mushroom penne 136
  macaroni cheese 121
  peperonata, pea & olive
    pasta 57
  prawn & chorizo spaghetti
    138
  spaghetti & meatballs 122
pastry, shortcrust 14, 206,
  216–18
patatas bravas 184
peanut butter & banana muffins
  22
peas
  peperonata, pea & olive
    pasta 57
  salmon, new potato & pea
    salad 76–7
  peas, yellow split
  pea soup with crispy
    chorizo croutons 176
pecan nuts
  decadent chocolate tart
    214
penne, creamy chicken, herb
  & mushroom 136
peppers

lemon & ginger
  chicken 190
peperonata, pea & olive
  pasta 57
sweet & sour chicken 189
whole roast jerk chicken
  147–8
pesto 230
  mint pesto dressing 76
pies
  apple & blackberry pie
    206–7
  fish pie 128
  shepherd's pie 127
pine nuts 230
  macaroni cheese 121
  mint pesto dressing 76
  pesto 230
pineapple
  mango & pineapple
    puddings 208
pizza bread 124
polenta 230
  chicken schnitzel with
    salsa verde 52
  cornbread 156
pork
  roast pork with potatoes,
    lemon, fennel &
    capers 144
potatoes
  baked leg of lamb with
    lemon, garlic &
    oregano 179
  chicken, artichoke &
    caper stew 149
  creamy garlic, herb &
    crispy bacon stuffed
    potatoes 126
  fish pie 128
  patatas bravas 184
  piquant potato wedges 119
  potato farls 26
  roast pork with potatoes,
    lemon, fennel &
    capers 144
  salmon, new potato & pea
    salad 76–7
  shepherd's pie 127
prawns
  grilled tiger prawns with
    avocado cream 182
  king prawn gazpacho 54
  prawn & chorizo spaghetti
    138

22

pumpkin pudding with spiced
  toffee sauce 222

q

quinoa 231
  grilled chermoula chicken
    with avocado quinoa
    salad 67
  quinoa tabbouleh 66

r

radishes
  watercress & radish salad
    with avocado dressing
    53
rapeseed oil 231
raspberry fizz 224
redcurrants
  gooseberry & redcurrant
    woodland crumble 213
rhubarb
  rhubarb & apple traybake
    102
  rhubarb & ginger sponge
    219
rice 225–6
  baked Italian chicken &
    rice 140
  chicken, fennel & raisin
    red rice salad 74
  hot-smoked salmon
    kedgeree with cashew
    sauce 29
  salmon & avocado sushi
    bowls 85
  seared chicken breasts
    with spiced coconut
    rice 137
  stir-fry jasmine rice 191
  rice, ground 228–9
  rice flour 231
  rice milk 231

s

St Clement's cake 105
salads
  carrot & orange salad 68
  chicken, fennel & raisin
    red rice salad 74
  chicken, roasted tomato &
    caper herb salad 69
  chicory, ham, sweet
    potato & sun-dried
    tomato salad 88

grilled chermoula chicken with avocado quinoa salad 67
quinoa tabbouleh 66
salmon, new potato & pea salad 76–7
spiced squash, avocado & mixed sprout salad 80
watercress & radish salad with avocado dressing 53
salmon
    sweet chilli & sesame salmon 150
    see also smoked salmon
salsas
    avocado salsa 194–6
    salsa verde 52
sauces
    cream sauce 166–7
    roasted tomato & basil sauce 120
    spiced toffee sauce 222
sausages 231
    sausage, lentil & sun-dried tomato cassoulet 158
scones
    butter bean & parsnip scones 86
    maple syrup scones 27
seeds, toasting 14
sesame oil, toasted 233
shepherd's pie 127
shortbread, lemon 41
shortcrust pastry 14, 206, 216–18
shortening, vegetable 233
smoked haddock
    fish pie 128
smoked salmon
    hot-smoked salmon kedgeree with cashew sauce 29
    salmon & avocado sushi bowls 85
    salmon, new potato & pea salad 76–7
smoothies 18–19
socca, roasted vegetable 71
soups
    butternut squash, lentil, honey & thyme soup 178
    king prawn gazpacho 54
    parsnip, chilli & lemon soup 89

pea soup with crispy chorizo croutons 176
    tomato & almond soup 185
spaghetti
    prawn & chorizo spaghetti 138
    spaghetti & meatballs 122
sprouts
    spiced squash, avocado & mixed sprout salad 80
squash
    baby squash with leeks & garlic & herb cheese 164
    butternut squash & tomato muffins 91
    butternut squash, lentil, honey & thyme soup 178
    pumpkin pudding with spiced toffee sauce 222
    spiced squash, avocado & mixed sprout salad 80
stews
    chestnut & chorizo stew 168
    chicken & preserved lemon tagine 165
    chicken, artichoke & caper stew 149
    Moroccan vegetable tagine 142
stocks 15, 232
strawberries
    strawberry & cream cupcakes 48
    strawberry ice cream 210
sunflower oil 232
sunflower seed butter 232–3
sunflower seed butter cookies 32
sweet potatoes
    chicory, ham, sweet potato & sun-dried tomato salad 88
    marmalade-baked chicken 134
    sweet potato & onion bhaji bites 162
    sweet potato bread 78
    whole roast jerk chicken 147–8
syrup sponge 221

t
tabbouleh, quinoa 66
tagines
    chicken & preserved lemon tagine 165
    Moroccan vegetable tagine 142
tahini 233
tamarind paste 233
tarts
    caramelised onion tart 61–2
    decadent chocolate tart 214
    French apple tart 216–18
    lemon & coconut tartlets 101
    lemon tart 202–4
toffee
    pumpkin pudding with spiced toffee sauce 222
tomatoes
    busy Boston baked beans 118
    butternut squash & tomato muffins 91
    chestnut & chorizo stew 168
    chicken & preserved lemon tagine 165
    chicken, roasted tomato & caper herb salad 69
    chicory, ham, sweet potato & sun-dried tomato salad 88
    chilli con carne 154
    king prawn gazpacho 54
    lamb, apricot and tahini meatballs 171
    marmalade-baked chicken 134
    patatas bravas 184
    pizza bread 124
    roasted tomato & basil sauce 120
    spaghetti & meatballs 122
    tomato & almond soup 185

v
vanilla
    vanilla bean paste 233
    vanilla bundt cake 109
    vanilla custard 213
    vanilla extract 233
    vanilla ice cream 205

vegetable shortening 233
vegetables
    grating 14
    Moroccan vegetable tagine 142
    roasted vegetable socca 71
    stock 232
    see also peppers, tomatoes etc

w
walnuts
    decadent chocolate tart 214
    poached chicken with walnut sauce 186–7
watercress & radish salad with avocado dressing 53

x
xanthan gum 233

y
yoghurt, coconut 227

thanks

This book is a celebration of all the amazing work, cooking, recipes, people, friendships and love that have shaped my life over the last few years. It is also a thank-you to all my readers (of both blog and book) and to those that have sent me such wonderful emails and messages in that time – thank you for reading.

I am especially grateful to all those people who have helped shaped this book. Thank you to Vicky Eribo and George Atsiaris at HarperCollins for their wonderful editorial work, invaluable encouragement and for both being quite so lovely. Thank you to Kate Parker, whose patient editing and enthusiasm for the subject was so gratefully received. Special thanks to Lucy Sykes-Thompson for her exceptional design skills and illustrative talent. Thank you to Martin Topping for creating such a wonderful design team and process – it has been a joy putting the book together with all of you.

Heartfelt thanks to Keiko Oikawa, whose stunning photography and style captured exactly the mood I had hoped for – truly perfect. To Liz Belton and Tabitha Hawkins for finding the most glorious and beautiful elements to add to the book – I loved everything. Endless thanks and love to Joss Herd, whose talent and food styling is a step above – you beauty! Thank you to Rosemary Scoular for her unstinting support and savvy.

Lastly, a heartfelt thank-you to all of my family and friends, to whom this book is dedicated; it would be a lesser creation without the love, support, conversation, company and friendship of you all.